God to the Rescue

Exodus

Kevin Perrotta

Gerald Darring

**Six Weeks
with the Bible
for Catholic Teens**

6

Exploring
God's Word

LOYOLAPRESS.

CHICAGO

LOYOLAPRESS.

3441 N. ASHLAND AVENUE
CHICAGO, ILLINOIS 60657
(800) 621-1008
WWW.LOYOLABOOKS.ORG

Nihil Obstat
Carolyn Osiek, RSCJ
Censor Deputatus
December 8, 2003

Imprimatur
Most Reverend Edwin M. Conway, D.D.
Vicar General
Archdiocese of Chicago
December 10, 2003

The *Nihil Obstat* and *Imprimatur* are official declarations that a book is free of doctrinal and moral error. No implication is contained therein that those who have granted the *Nihil Obstat* and *Imprimatur* agree with the content, opinions, or statements expressed.

20–21 From *Harriet Tubman* by Rebecca Price Janney (Minneapolis: Bethany House Publishers, 1999).

44–45 From "Newman Center holds Passover Seder Meal" by Kelley Kepler. *Superior Catholic Herald* (April 17, 2003).

56–57 From an earlier version of Mary Anne Beggs's story, which appeared in *God's Word Today* (July 1998), 41. Used with permission of *God's Word Today.*

81 From "The Youthful Heart" by Yves Congar, O.P., in *Revue des Jeunes,* January 1935.

89–90 Excerpts from the English translation of the writings of John Chrysostom and St. Cyprian from *The Liturgy of the Hours* © 1974, International Committee on English in the Liturgy, Inc. All rights reserved.

Cover and Interior Design: Th!nk Design Group

ISBN 0-8294-2051-7

Printed in the United States of America
04 05 06 07 08 Bang 5 4 3 2 1

Contents

How to Use This Guide

You might compare this booklet to a short visit to a national park. The park is so large that you could spend months, even years, getting to know it. But a brief visit, if carefully planned, can be worthwhile. In a few hours you can drive through the park and pull over at a handful of sites. At each stop you can get out of the car, take a short trail through the woods, listen to the wind blowing in the trees, and get a feel for the place.

In this booklet we'll travel through portions of the book of Exodus. We will take a leisurely walk through our targeted readings, thinking carefully about what we are reading and what it means for our lives today. After each discussion, we'll get back in the car and take the highway to the next stop. The "Between Discussions" pages summarize the portions of Exodus that we will pass along the way.

This guide provides everything you need to explore these portions of Exodus in six discussions—or to do a six-part exploration on your own. The introduction will prepare you to get the most out of your reading. The weekly sections provide explanations that highlight what the words of Exodus mean for us today. Equally important, each section supplies questions that will launch you into fruitful discussion, helping you both to explore Exodus for yourself and to learn from one another. If you're using the booklet by yourself, the questions will spur your personal reflection.

Each discussion is meant to be a *guided discovery*.

Guided ~ None of us is equipped to read the Bible without help. We read the Bible *for* ourselves but not *by* ourselves. Scripture was written to be understood and applied in and with the Church. So each week "A Guide to the Reading," drawing on the work of both modern biblical scholars and Christian writers of the past, supplies background and explanations. The guide will help you grasp the message of Exodus. Think of it as a friendly park ranger who points out noteworthy details and explains what you're looking at so you can appreciate things for yourself.

Discovery ~ The purpose is for *you* to interact with the book of Exodus. "Questions for a Closer Look" is a tool to help you dig into the text and examine it carefully. "Questions for Application" will help you discern what the words of Exodus mean for your life here and now. Each week concludes with an "Approach to Prayer" section that helps you respond to God's Word. The supplementary "Living Tradition" and "Saints in the Making" sections offer the thoughts and experiences of Christians past and present in order to show you what Exodus has meant to others—so that you can consider what it might mean for you.

If you are using this booklet for individual study, pay special attention to the questions provided for each week (Warm-Up Questions, Questions for a Closer Look, Questions for Application). One advantage of individual study is that you can take all the time you need to consider each question. I also suggest that you read the entire book of Exodus; you will find that the "Between Discussions" pages will help you understand the portions of Exodus not covered in this guide. Take your time making your way through Exodus and this accompanying booklet: let your reading be an opportunity for these stories to become God's words to you.

Israel's Deliverance— and Ours

The book of Exodus surely ranks high on the list of most exciting pieces of literature ever written. The account has all the elements of a great drama: conflict, emotion, suspense, heroism. A ragtag group of people, under the leadership of one of their own, frees themselves from slavery to a cruel oppressor. God opens up the sea, saving them from certain destruction, while the army of their pursuers is devastated by the returning waters. They find themselves in a bleak desert, a crowd of former slaves forced to learn quickly how to survive in the wilderness. They were often disgruntled at the growing pains of their newly won freedom, but in spite of everything, they became a nation covenanted to God, challenged to obey the laws God writes for them on stone tablets.

Movies have been made about the Exodus story of the Israelites' escape from slavery, but Hollywood was not the first to see the dramatic potential of the book of Exodus. More than a century before Christ, a Jewish playwright named Ezekiel (not the Old Testament prophet) wrote a play based on the book in the style of the Greek tragedies. The drama included an eyewitness account of the miracle at the Red Sea by a surviving member of the Egyptian army:

> God was their defense, for when they reached the farther shore a mighty wave gushed forth hard by us, so that one of us in terror cried, "Flee back before the hands of the Most High. To them he offers assistance, but to us, most wretched men, he works destruction." The sea-path flooded, all our company was lost.

A millennium later, a Christian poet recast the story in the form of an Anglo-Saxon epic:

> Then Moses spoke with a loud voice before the multitude: "Look now, dearest of people, with your eyes and behold a

marvel! The waves rise up; the waters form a rampart-wall. The sea is thrust aside. . . . Well I know Almighty God has shown you mercy. Most haste is best now, so that you may escape the clutch of foes, since God has reared a rampart of the red sea-streams."

Dramatic as it is, however, Exodus is much more than entertainment. Both Jews and Christians base their faith on the events described in Exodus. References to God's leading the Israelites from slavery to freedom occur more than 75 times throughout the Old Testament. The Exodus continues to echo in the New Testament accounts of Jesus' death and resurrection.

The Exodus was God's greatest act of deliverance in the Old Testament. God freed the Israelites from slavery through the Exodus. He established a relationship with them, and prepared them to live together as a people. The Exodus is the major turning point in Jewish history. Jews view everything in their history from the standpoint of these saving events. The events of the Exodus, then, are not just things that happened a long time ago. They are living realities that remain ever present. Each generation hands down to the next the memory of the Exodus and the assurance that the God of the Exodus still acts today. The principal Jewish feast, Passover, commemorates Israel's liberation from slavery in Egypt. The Passover meal is celebrated year after year as a means of remembering and reliving these defining events.

Israel's deliverance from Egypt holds an essential place in the history not only of Jews but of Christians as well. God's promise in Genesis to rescue humankind from the forces of sin and alienation unfolds in the story of the Exodus. This story of salvation is *one* story, and the faith of Jews and Christians alike is rooted in these saving actions of God. Thus, as Christians, we share the Passover perspective of the Jews, our elder brothers and sisters in faith. But we celebrate a further deliverance, one we recognize as the fulfillment of God's plan of salvation: Christ's freeing all men and women from sin and death through his death and resurrection. Jesus himself linked Passover to his passing over from earthly to risen life. In a radiant vision of himself that he granted to his disciples, in which he appeared with Moses and Elijah, he conversed about "his departure," literally his *exodus,* "which he was about to accomplish at Jerusalem" (Luke 9:31). Saint Paul also spoke of Jesus' death and resurrection in terms of the Exodus: "For our paschal lamb, Christ, has been sacrificed" (1 Corinthians 5:7). Thus each Easter is a celebration of the Christian Passover.

Christians see the Exodus as a foreshadowing of what God was going to accomplish through Jesus' death and resurrection. This fits with the Church's approach to the Old Testament. From its earliest days, the Church has viewed the Old Testament as the record of God's unfolding the first steps of a plan of salvation fulfilled in Christ.

Thus, the early Christians understood the Exodus story on two levels. On the first level, the events show God rescuing the Israelites so that he might draw them into a relationship with him. On the second level, the actions in Exodus point forward to God's greatest action, accomplished through his Son, Jesus.

There is, then, a relationship between Passover in the Old Testament and Christ's death and resurrection in the New Testament. God's sparing the people of Israel from death on the night of the Passover is a prefigurement of God's sparing us from eternal destruction through Jesus' death. The lamb eaten at Passover prefigures Christ, the Lamb of God. The Passover lamb's blood on the doorposts of the Israelites' houses is an image of Christ's blood shed on the cross: just as the lamb's blood brought the Israelites' safety, so Christ's blood preserves us from eternal death by removing our sins.

Exodus, then, is not just about God's actions for Israel long ago; it is also about God's activity in our lives as followers of Christ. In reading about the rescue of the Israelite slaves, we can learn about God's saving love for us in Christ. The way God sustained the Israelites in the wilderness reminds us of some of the sacraments of the Church. For example, our immersion into Christ's death and life through the water of Baptism harkens back to the Israelites' passing through the water of the Red Sea. God's provision of manna offers us an image of the Eucharist, the heavenly bread by which we are nourished—Christ's body and blood. Thus, as we read about God's rescue of his people Israel, we can ask the Holy Spirit to help us understand better our own personal salvation history. We can ask ourselves how we have experienced being rescued from the grip of sin, how we have discovered the personal presence of Jesus as he lives with us in the new covenant he has made through his death and resurrection.

From before the time of Jesus, Jewish tradition held that Moses wrote the entire Pentateuch, the first five books of the Bible (Genesis, Exodus, Leviticus, Numbers, Deuteronomy). For centuries this was also the general view among Christians. We now know that Exodus was composed over a long period of time and may not have been put into its final form until around the fifth century B.C., some eight centuries after Moses—although Moses may have written portions of it (17:14; 24:4; 34:27; all citations in this booklet refer to Exodus unless otherwise noted). The tradition of Moses' authorship of the Pentateuch does, however, reflect Moses' central role in the formation of the Israelite people.

Over a period of several hundred years, the nucleus of the Exodus story—the departure from Egypt, the desert journey, the covenant and the giving of the law at Mount Sinai—was passed down by word of mouth and then gradually began to be written down. The early accounts were changed later on to express new experiences and a new understanding of God. The process of editing does not show itself in the text, and we can only guess at who actually composed it. In any case, the authors tied together different versions of events, reflecting different stages in Israel's life as a nation. It is obvious from the different literary styles in Exodus that poets, lawyers, historians, and priests all contributed to the development of the text we have.

Once we understand the editorial process, we can see why the text of Exodus repeats and even seems to contradict itself. The editors wanted to be faithful to all the ways people remembered the story, so they kept all the different features, and in so doing, actually made the book more powerful. At the same time, the final text presents a clear story line that progresses chronologically from the death of Joseph, through Israel's oppression and deliverance, to the people's encounter with God at Mount Sinai and the giving of the Law.

Understanding the editorial process also helps us deal with the question of what really happened. The authors did not have available to them reliable written records. Instead, they had stories that had been passed down from one generation to the next. As the stories were handed on, they were adapted so as to focus attention on God's presence in the historical events. The authors then combined these stories with some legendary material, instructions for worship, moral teaching, and other material. The result is a book that has little in common with what we would consider a history book.

Should we expect to find accurate history in the book of Exodus? No, but that does not mean that Exodus is not true. We have to judge the authors' work on the basis of what they were trying to communicate. The authors were not trying to write a modern history book. They wanted to tell about what God did to save the Israelites and make them into a people. They hoped to reveal what God is like and what kind of relationship he wishes to have with people. They interpreted the Exodus story in terms of God intervening on behalf of the oppressed Israelites. Was their portrait of God true? Did they accurately portray God's intentions for his people? The answer is an emphatic yes.

We are still curious, of course, about what really happened, and scholars are debating the issue. Some think that the pharaoh who appears in the Exodus story is Rameses II, who reigned through most of the 13th century B.C. We know that Rameses II undertook vast building projects in the Nile Delta and that he used foreign slaves in these projects. However, there is no mention of Israelites in Egypt in any of the Egyptian records we have.

There is no indication outside the Bible that the Israelites spent time in the wilderness. There can be no doubt, however, about the existence of Israel as a people. *Some* events must have occurred to bring into existence this people who believed that God made a covenant with them and gave them a law on which to pattern their way of life. The best way to explain the existence of Israel is to use the Exodus account: slaves escaped from Egypt; they saw this as an act of God; they then experienced God revealing himself to them in the wilderness of Sinai, drawing them into a relationship with him.

Hard Times

Warm-Up Questions

1 How recently did your family come to this country?
- ○ I'm an immigrant myself.
- ○ My grandparents were immigrants who came here and struggled to make good.
- ○ My family has been in this country as long as any of us can remember.
- ○ I know little about my family's history but would like to learn more.

2 What do you think it would be like to live in another country or move to an unfamiliar city? Would you find it hard to adapt to your new surroundings?

3 Which of these social evils in the world today most concerns you: hunger, discrimination, war, homelessness, child abuse?

Opening the Bible

Exodus 1:1—2:10

Good Old Days

[1:1] These are the names of the sons of Israel who came to Egypt
with Jacob, each with his household: [2] Reuben, Simeon, Levi, and
Judah, [3] Issachar, Zebulun, and Benjamin, [4] Dan and Naphtali,
Gad and Asher. [5] The total number of people born to Jacob was
seventy. Joseph was already in Egypt. [6] Then Joseph died, and all
his brothers, and that whole generation. [7] But the Israelites were
fruitful and prolific; they multiplied and grew exceedingly strong,
so that the land was filled with them.

Life Gets Tough

[8] Now a new king arose over Egypt, who did not know Joseph.
[9] He said to his people, "Look, the Israelite people are more
numerous and more powerful than we. [10] Come, let us deal
shrewdly with them, or they will increase and, in the event of war,
join our enemies and fight against us and escape from the land."
[11] Therefore they set taskmasters over them to oppress them with
forced labor. They built supply cities, Pithom and Rameses, for
Pharaoh. [12] But the more they were oppressed, the more they
multiplied and spread, so that the Egyptians came to dread the
Israelites. [13] The Egyptians became ruthless in imposing tasks on
the Israelites, [14] and made their lives bitter with hard service in
mortar and brick and in every kind of field labor. They were
ruthless in all the tasks that they imposed on them.
[15] The king of Egypt said to the Hebrew midwives, one of
whom was named Shiphrah and the other Puah, [16] "When you act
as midwives to the Hebrew women, and see them on the
birthstool, if it is a boy, kill him; but if it is a girl, she shall live."
[17] But the midwives feared God; they did not do as the king of
Egypt commanded them, but they let the boys live. [18] So the king
of Egypt summoned the midwives and said to them, "Why have
you done this, and allowed the boys to live?" [19] The midwives said
to Pharaoh, "Because the Hebrew women are not like the
Egyptian women; for they are vigorous and give birth before the

midwife comes to them." [20] So God dealt well with the midwives; and the people multiplied and became very strong. [21] And because the midwives feared God, he gave them families. [22] Then Pharaoh commanded all his people, "Every boy that is born to the Hebrews you shall throw into the Nile, but you shall let every girl live."

Hey, There's a Baby in That Basket!

[2:1] Now a man from the house of Levi went and married a Levite woman. [2] The woman conceived and bore a son; and when she saw that he was a fine baby, she hid him three months. [3] When she could hide him no longer she got a papyrus basket for him, and plastered it with bitumen and pitch; she put the child in it and placed it among the reeds on the bank of the river. [4] His sister stood at a distance, to see what would happen to him.

[5] The daughter of Pharaoh came down to bathe at the river, while her attendants walked beside the river. She saw the basket among the reeds and sent her maid to bring it. [6] When she opened it, she saw the child. He was crying, and she took pity on him. "This must be one of the Hebrews' children," she said. [7] Then his sister said to Pharaoh's daughter, "Shall I go and get you a nurse from the Hebrew women to nurse the child for you?" [8] Pharaoh's daughter said to her, "Yes." So the girl went and called the child's mother. [9] Pharaoh's daughter said to her, "Take this child and nurse it for me, and I will give you your wages." So the woman took the child and nursed it. [10] When the child grew up, she brought him to Pharaoh's daughter, and she took him as her son. She named him Moses, "because," she said, "I drew him out of the water."

Questions for a Closer Look

1 Reread these verses: 1:8–10,15–16,22. What picture of Pharaoh would you draw from these passages? What does this tell you about the seriousness of the Israelites' situation?

2 The Egyptians' policies against the Hebrews develop in stages. How many stages can be distinguished in this reading? As the Egyptians' policies become harsher, do they also become more successful?

3 In 1:17 what does the word *feared* mean? What was the midwives' attitude toward God? toward Pharaoh's decree?

4 Identify all the women who play a role in this reading. What trait(s) do they have in common?

5 Why do you think Pharaoh's daughter defied her father's orders?

6 What indications does this reading give that God is concerned for the Israelites?

A Guide to the Reading

The Hebrew name for the book we call Exodus is "These are the names." The same words are used towards the end of Genesis, and both times the words introduce a list of those who came to Egypt with Jacob. The two books are thus connected, highlighting the fact that God continued to work from one period to the next. God's plan unfolds throughout the Bible, a great plan for the good of men and women that reaches its fulfillment in Jesus Christ.

Genesis describes the creation of the world and tells how the first humans brought unhappiness on themselves and their descendants by refusing to obey God. Then Genesis tells how God started a plan to restore people's relationship with him. The first phase of the plan involved a family: Abraham and Sarah, their son, Isaac, and his wife, Rebekah, followed by their son Jacob, his wives, and their twelve sons (named in 1:2–5). Genesis focused on the family circle. In Exodus this family will move out into the wider arena of world history. The great family leaders of earlier generations will now be followed by a great deliverer and lawgiver, Moses. Exodus begins with the story of his birth.

Jacob and his family originally came to Egypt to get food during a famine. God assured Jacob: "Do not be afraid to go down to Egypt, for I will make of you a great nation there" (Genesis 46:3). The family prospered in Egypt under the protection of Jacob's son Joseph, who had risen to high rank in the Egyptian government. Jacob's descendants thrived and grew in the land to which they had come as refugees (1:7). Thus God kept the promise he made to Jacob and earlier to Abraham: "I will make your offspring as numerous as the stars of heaven" (Genesis 22:17).

God had told Abraham in advance about the slavery of Abraham's descendants and God's intervention. "Your offspring shall be aliens in a land that is not theirs, and shall be slaves there, and they shall be oppressed for 400 years; but I will bring judgment on the nation that they serve, and afterward they shall come out with great possessions" (Genesis 15:13–14). The prediction of distress was fulfilled, as Abraham's descendants find themselves in a brutally degrading and life-threatening situation. We know the rest of God's promise, of course, so we may expect that God will hear their desperate cries and provide a solution to their situation.

Pharaoh was not a personal name but simply a way of referring to the kings of Egypt; in Egyptian it means "great house" or "palace." Exodus never speaks of the Egyptian king by his personal name, and this makes it easy to see Pharaoh as a faceless symbol of oppression. Pharaoh represents the human and spiritual forces, including Satan, that make slaves of us. Indeed, the entire story of Exodus can be read both literally and symbolically. On the literal level, it speaks about the plight of the Israelites, who lived in Egypt as slaves under a cruel tyrant. On the symbolic level, it speaks about all of us, who are slaves to sin and separated from God's grace. We can also see in Pharaoh's namelessness a symbol of something in ourselves, of our dark tendencies to act at times as Pharaoh did, blind to God's will for us.

The book of Exodus describes a struggle between Israel's God and Pharaoh, who was worshipped as a god by his subjects. Pharaoh seems far the stronger at first. He appears to exercise unlimited power: he imposes slavery and orders genocide. The Israelites' situation seems hopeless in the face of his power. Their God seems powerless or absent. God, however, sets in motion a plan to raise up a liberator. The baby Moses is put in a basket—the same Hebrew word was used for Noah's ark (Genesis 6:14). Moses' basket is like Noah's boat: God's instrument of salvation from the waters. The meaning given to Moses' name, "drawn from the water," speaks of God's saving power. As we will see, it will be through Moses that the people of Israel will gain freedom and enter into a covenant with God. Through the baby in the basket, God will demonstrate who is really Lord.

Questions for Application

1 When do people feel pressured to do wrong—for example, to cheat or to lie or to close their eyes to injustice? Have you ever been able to bring justice into an unjust situation? What prompts people to make the right choices and act courageously in such situations?

2 The midwives worked together to thwart Pharaoh's plans to have all the male babies killed. What can an individual do to fight injustice, and, when necessary, to work with others to bring about justice?

3 Pharaoh's daughter rescued the baby Moses. Do you know someone who has been rescued by another person? What happened?

4 When Moses' mother and sister placed him in the basket, they could do nothing more to save him; they could only trust God to act. In what areas of our lives do we most need to trust God to act?

5 The Israelites came as strangers in need to Egypt. Who are the newcomers in your school or parish or neighborhood? How could you reach out to them and offer friendship and help?

6 Earlier you were asked to identify the social evil you care about most. What are some things you might do to bring about justice, or at least to alleviate the injustice?

Approach to Prayer

If you wish, share briefly with the group a need you or someone you knows has for God's help. Then take a moment to pray in silence for the needs of everyone in the room. Close your time together with the Our Father.

Saints in the Making

Way Down in Egypt's Land

Through the centuries, the Israelites' oppression under their ruthless taskmasters in Egypt became a symbol of the many forms of bondage and injustice suffered by human beings. Many of the religious songs popular among slaves in the American South expressed their yearning for freedom as well as their longing for heaven. These Negro spirituals brought hope to men and women familiar with backbreaking work and lashings. "Go Down, Moses" was a particular favorite.

> When Israel was in Egypt's land, Let my people go,
> Oppressed so hard they could not stand, Let my people go.
>
> *Chorus:* Go down, Moses, Way down in Egypt's land,
> Tell old Pharaoh, To let my people go.
>
> No more shall they in bondage toil, Let my people go,
> Let them come out with Egypt's spoil, Let my people go. *Chorus*

Some former slaves saw Harriet Tubman as the Moses of this song. Tubman made her own escape from slavery in 1849. Hiding by day and following the North Star at night, she reached the free state of Pennsylvania. "I looked at my hands to see if I was the same person, now that I was free," she recalled. "There was such a glory over everything. The sun came up like gold through the trees and over the fields, and I felt like I was in heaven."

Once she was free, Tubman determined to rescue as many other slaves as possible. "To this solemn resolution I came; I was free, and they should be free also," she later said. "I would make a home for them in the North and, the Lord helping me, I would bring them all there."

During the decade before the Civil War, Tubman made 19 journeys back into "Egypt's land"—the American South. She led more than 300 slaves to freedom through the network of helpers called the Underground Railroad. By God's grace, she declared, "I never ran my 'train' off the track, and I never lost a passenger."

Between
Discussions

The Bible does not tell us much about Moses' early life except for a few details about his family background and education. His mother was Jochebed and his father was Amram. They belonged to the tribe of Levi and had at least two other children, Aaron and Miriam. We know nothing else about them except that Jochebed became the paid wet nurse for Moses until he was adopted by Pharaoh's daughter and taken into her household. Pharaoh had ordered all the Hebrew male babies to be killed, and yet he ended up with one of them as his adopted grandson—though we might wonder whether, in such a great household, Pharaoh was even aware of the child.

Exodus gives no information about Moses the teenager, although in the New Testament Saint Stephen tells us that Moses was "instructed in all the wisdom of the Egyptians and was powerful in his words and deeds" (Acts 7:22). His instruction must have included religious, civil, and military matters.

The education he gained at the Egyptian court undoubtedly helped him learn what he needed to know in order to confront the next Pharaoh.

Moses was raised apart from his Hebrew community. It was not until he was well into adulthood, then, that he began to be affected by his awareness of being a Hebrew. As Saint Stephen recounted, "When he was forty years old, it came into his heart to visit his relatives, the Israelites" (Acts 7:23). It was then that he first took action against his people's oppression. He murdered an Egyptian who was beating a Hebrew and as a result had to flee from Pharaoh's wrath (2:11–15; Acts 7:24–29).

Moses settled down, probably in the Sinai Peninsula, married, and became a shepherd (2:15–22; 3:1). During these long years he matured in character and he probably thought a lot about his relatives back in Egypt. He named his son Gershom—which means "resident alien" in Hebrew— showing his awareness that he was "an alien residing in a foreign land" (2:22). He may have daydreamed about visiting his own people and seeing how they were doing, but he probably did not see himself coming to their rescue. After all, what could one man do against the strength of Egypt?

A long time passed. Then, one day while Moses was herding his sheep, he saw a bush burning, but not consumed by the flames. What did this strange sight mean? Moses was about to be drawn into God's plan for delivering the Israelites (2:23–25).

The stories of Moses and Jesus were similar in many ways. Both Moses and Jesus were born into a people who were suffering under repressive rule. They both survived attempts to have all the male infants killed. Exodus tells us nothing about Moses' youthful years, and, except for the incident among the teachers in the Temple, the Gospels tell us nothing of Jesus' boyhood. Both Moses and Jesus were called by God for a great purpose. They both spent time in the desert preparing for their missions: Moses as a shepherd in Midian for 40 years, Jesus in his 40-day fast in the desert. They were both misunderstood by those who were closest to them: Moses by his brother and sister, Jesus by his family and his disciples. Finally, the people of Israel were freed from slavery and led to the Promised Land under the leadership of Moses, while through Jesus all of us are redeemed from sin and the way to heaven is opened.

Everything we know about Moses comes from the Bible. There are, however, many legends about Moses in Jewish lore and rabbinical literature. Such tales are purely imaginative, but they reflect how important Moses is for the Jews. He was the liberator of Israel, its leader, lawgiver, intercessor, and mediator with God. Judaism is often called the Mosaic faith. Even today Moses' influence is felt in the religious life, moral concerns, and social ethics of Western civilization.

God Calling

Warm-Up Questions

1 Which of these experiences would do the most to make you feel like you were standing on holy ground?
- ○ Being in a cathedral with soaring Gothic arches and shining stained-glass windows
- ○ Watching a gorgeous sunset from a lofty mountain
- ○ Holding a newborn infant
- ○ Praying before the Blessed Sacrament
- ○ Other

2 How would you react to this awesome sense of God's presence and holiness?
- ○ Gasp in wonder and exclaim, "Ah!"
- ○ Kneel down in adoration
- ○ Cover your eyes in the face of such beauty
- ○ Feel humble and unworthy

3 Does your name have a special meaning (for example, *Peter* means "rock," *Margaret* means "daisy" or "pearl")? If you had to pick a different name for yourself, what would it be?

Opening the Bible

What's Happened

Although Moses grows up in Pharaoh's household, he recognizes the Israelites as his people. On one occasion, he is troubled to see a fellow Hebrew being beaten by an Egyptian overseer and comes to the man's defense, killing the Egyptian (2:11–15). He is obliged to flee from Egypt and settles in Midian (probably in the dry Sinai Peninsula), where he marries, raises a family, and tends sheep (2:15–22). Many years pass. All the while, the Israelites suffer oppression. Finally, God is ready to act.

THE READING

Exodus 2:23—3:17

God Hears the People's Cry

2:23 After a long time the king of Egypt died. The Israelites groaned under their slavery, and cried out. Out of the slavery their cry for help rose up to God. 24 God heard their groaning, and God remembered his covenant with Abraham, Isaac, and Jacob. 25 God looked upon the Israelites, and God took notice of them.

What's the Story with This Bush?

3:1 Moses was keeping the flock of his father-in-law Jethro, the priest of Midian; he led his flock beyond the wilderness, and came to Horeb, the mountain of God. 2 There the angel of the LORD* appeared to him in a flame of fire out of a bush; he looked, and the bush was blazing, yet it was not consumed. 3 Then Moses said, "I must turn aside and look at this great sight, and see why the bush is not burned up." 4 When the LORD saw that he had turned aside to see, God called to him out of the bush, "Moses, Moses!" And he said, "Here I am." 5 Then he said, "Come no closer! Remove the sandals from your feet, for the place on which you are

---

* By printing Lord in capital letters the translators indicate that the Hebrew text does not use the word for "lord" but the proper name of God (see this week's Supplement for Individual Reading).

standing is holy ground." [6] He said further, "I am the God of your father, the God of Abraham, the God of Isaac, and the God of Jacob." And Moses hid his face, for he was afraid to look at God.

Who, Me?

[7] Then the LORD said, "I have observed the misery of my people who are in Egypt; I have heard their cry on account of their taskmasters. Indeed, I know their sufferings, [8] and I have come down to deliver them from the Egyptians, and to bring them up out of that land to a good and broad land, a land flowing with milk and honey, to the country of the Canaanites, the Hittites, the Amorites, the Perizzites, the Hivites, and the Jebusites. [9] The cry of the Israelites has now come to me; I have also seen how the Egyptians oppress them. [10] So come, I will send you to Pharaoh to bring my people, the Israelites, out of Egypt." [11] But Moses said to God, "Who am I that I should go to Pharaoh, and bring the Israelites out of Egypt?" [12] He said, "I will be with you; and this shall be the sign for you that it is I who sent you: when you have brought the people out of Egypt, you shall worship God on this mountain."

God Reveals His Name

[13] But Moses said to God, "If I come to the Israelites and say to them, 'The God of your ancestors has sent me to you,' and they ask me, 'What is his name?' what shall I say to them?" [14] God said to Moses, "I AM WHO I AM." He said further, "Thus you shall say to the Israelites, 'I AM has sent me to you.'" [15] God also said to Moses, "Thus you shall say to the Israelites, 'The LORD, the God of your ancestors, the God of Abraham, the God of Isaac, and the God of Jacob, has sent me to you':

    This is my name forever,
    and this my title for all generations.
[16] Go and assemble the elders of Israel, and say to them, 'The LORD, the God of your ancestors, the God of Abraham, of Isaac, and of Jacob, has appeared to me, saying: I have given heed to you and to what has been done to you in Egypt. [17] I declare that I will bring you up out of the misery of Egypt, to the land of the Canaanites, the Hittites, the Amorites, the Perizzites, the Hivites, and the Jebusites, a land flowing with milk and honey.'"

Questions for a Closer Look

1 What do you think the author means in 2:24 when he writes that God "remembered" his covenant with Abraham, Isaac, and Jacob?

2 Find the verses where God calls himself the "God of Abraham, Isaac, and Jacob." Why do you think God speaks about himself this way?

3 What do you think is the meaning of the extraordinary appearance of the bush?

4 What does Moses do to acknowledge that he is in the presence of God? What do his actions tell us about him?

5 How would you describe Moses' response when God tells him to go to Pharaoh as the deliverer of the Israelites?

6 Why did Moses ask God what his name is?

A Guide to the Reading

Moses must have been very surprised when God appeared to him in the burning bush. He had always been a family man and a peaceful shepherd, minding his own business in Midian, far away from the Egypt of his earlier years. He may have even tried to forget the distress of his people in Egypt. He might have thought that there was nothing he could do about it anyway. But God had other things in mind for him.

God has used many imperfect people, such as Moses, to advance his plans for the world. Moses had a pagan upbringing and he had killed a person, so he was not exactly the kind of person you might think would make a servant of God. But God has often shown his power by working through human weakness, making saints out of sinners. God often picks someone who seems like the wrong person for the job, people like Jonah, who tried to run away from God's commission to preach to the Ninevites; or David, who committed adultery and murder; or Peter, who denied that he knew Jesus. But God called each of them, in spite of their failings, to play an important part in his plans. Now he is going to take the unlikely Moses and make him into the liberator of Israel.

Moses shepherded his flocks in the wilderness, and later he would lead his people through the same wilderness. His being a shepherd may even have helped get him ready to be a leader of his people. Notice that God's call comes to him while he is doing his daily work. It often happens that an insight into our vocation comes when we least expect it. That is how God's call came to Abraham, to the prophet Isaiah, and to the apostle Paul. Moses responded willingly to God, just as Abraham and Samuel and many others have done.

When Moses questions whether he was the right person for the task, he was also doing what many other reluctant people have done (see, for example, Gideon in the book of Judges, 6:11–24). Moses asks God, "Who am I that I should go to Pharaoh, and bring the Israelites out of Egypt?" (3:11). Most of God's servants have felt that they were unworthy or incapable of carrying out the mission that God asked of them. But God reassures Moses with the promise " I will be with you" (3:12), and he gives Moses what he will need to carry out his mission.

The bush that was on fire but not burning up caught Moses' attention. He came closer to get a better look, but God warned him not to come too close, for he was on holy ground. In many cultures, taking off one's shoes is still a mark of respect for God: Muslims take off their shoes before entering a mosque, and in India Christians do the same before entering churches. Moses knew he was in the presence of something magnificent and hid his face, afraid to look at God.

Moses' ancestors had invoked God under various names, for example, *El Shaddai,* usually translated "God Almighty." But with God's appearance in the burning bush, there begins a new phase of history and with it, a new name for God. God is about to move his plans forward in a dramatic way. He will keep his promise to Abraham's family to bring their descendants "to a good and broad land, a land flowing with milk and honey" (3:8). This Promised Land will be the ultimate goal of Israel's deliverance from slavery in Egypt. It will also prefigure our ultimate goal of heaven. As he launches this new stage of his plan in history, God reveals his own personal name to Moses. "I AM WHO I AM" is a name that speaks of God's sovereignty, power, and freedom. This new name for God is revealed to Moses and Israel as they are about to enter a dangerous and difficult phase, and it is an assurance of God's power to fulfill his promises (see this week's Supplement for Individual Reading).

Questions for Application

1 How does God work through the ordinary events of our lives to make himself present to us? What is something we can do to make ourselves more alert to God's interventions in our lives and his word to us day by day?

2 Have you ever experienced the awesome greatness of God in nature? in church? in personal prayer? with other people? What effect can such an experience have on us?

3 Do you believe that God knows about our problems and helps us the way he helped the Israelites? What are some ways in which people experience God's care and love?

4 Moses objected when God told him to go to Pharaoh. How would you respond if you felt that God was calling you to do something that seemed impossible?

5 God sent Moses back to his fellow Israelites to tell them that God had given him a message of hope for them. There seem to be many people in the world today who are caught in seemingly hopeless situations. How can we communicate to them a message of hope?

6 What titles for God do you use when you approach him in prayer? Which titles for God are you most comfortable with? Why?

Approach to Prayer

If you wish, mention to the group an area of your life where you are in need of greater trust in God's care for you or a clearer sense of God's direction. Conclude with a few minutes of conversational prayer, expressing trust in God and asking him to meet one another's needs.

──── or ────

Spend some time in silent prayer so that you can ask God for the comfort or direction that you need for situations you are facing in your life. Then pray along silently as one member of the group prays aloud this prayer written by the Venerable Charles de Foucauld expressing trust in God:

*My Father, I put myself in your
hands. I abandon myself to you.
Do with me what you will.
Whatever you may do with me, I
thank you. I am prepared for
anything. I accept everything,
provided your will is fulfilled in
me and in all creatures. I ask for
nothing more, my God. I place my
soul in your hands. I give it to
you, my God, with all the love of
my heart, because I love you. For
me it is a necessity of love, this gift
of myself, this placing of myself
into your hands without reserve in
boundless confidence because you
are my Father.*

A Living Tradition

I Am Who I Am

Before the incident of the burning bush, the Israelites would refer to God using the ordinary Hebrew word for God. They would also use a title describing God or God's relationship with people, for example, *El Shaddai* ("God Almighty") or "the God of our fathers." When God told Moses his "personal" name at the burning bush, he was giving a great gift to the Israelites. He was revealing to them his divine Person.

The Hebrew of Exodus 3:14 may be translated "I AM WHO I AM" or "I WILL BE WHAT I WILL BE." For many centuries it has been translated "I AM THE ONE WHO IS." We use the first person pronoun, "I," because God is speaking, but in the Hebrew portions of the Old Testament, the third person pronoun, "He," is used. The translation then comes out as "HE WHO CAUSES TO BE." We should not, therefore, see God's name as a statement about God's absolute being or unchanging existence. God's name should tell us something about God as creator, the one who intervenes in human history, the one who saves with his presence. Obviously, no translation will be good enough to say all this, and in the end we must accept God's name as a mystery. God is so far above everything that we can understand that we cannot even name him adequately.

Vowels are normally not written in Hebrew, but in texts of the Bible vowel markings are added. In Jewish tradition, however, God's name is written either without vowel markings or with the vowel markings of the Hebrew word for "lord." This tells the reader to say *Lord* instead of pronouncing the divine name that Jews never utter because of their reverence for God.

The four Hebrew consonants of the divine name are called the Tetragrammaton, which means "the four letters." Scholars conjecture that the Tetragrammaton was pronounced "Yahweh." Most English translators render the Tetragrammaton as "Lord." The form "Jehovah" is based on a misunderstanding; it results from pronouncing the consonants of the Tetragrammaton with the vowels of the Hebrew word for "lord."

Moses was hesitant to accept the role of liberator of Israel; in fact, he tried hard to get out of the job. His first excuse was that the Israelites would not listen to him or believe that God had sent him (4:1). God responded by giving him some extraordinary signs that he could use to convince the people (4:2–9). So Moses came up with another excuse, saying that he was a poor speaker (4:10), but God assured him that he would teach him what to say. Finally, Moses simply tried to beg off: "O my Lord, please send someone else" (4:13). At this point, God got angry (4:14), but he agreed to let Moses' brother Aaron help him because Aaron was a fluent speaker. Moses would tell Aaron what God said, and Aaron would declare it to the people (4:16).

Moses and Aaron came into Egypt, told the Israelites that the Lord had spoken to them, and showed them the signs that God had given them to perform. The people now realized that God *had* seen their misery and was finally about to act (4:29–31). But when the two brothers told Pharaoh to let the Israelites go and worship their God in the desert, he objected. "Who is the LORD," he said, "that I should heed him and let Israel go?" (5:2). He did not want to lose Egypt's free labor source, so he asked, "Why are you taking the people away from their work?" (5:4). With that, Pharaoh ordered that the Israelites would have to produce their quota of bricks without being given the straw needed to make them. *Gathering their own straw,* Pharaoh reasoned, *will keep them too busy to listen to that troublemaker Moses.*

So things got worse rather than better when the Israelites started to do God's will. But God had just begun to act, and he promised again to deliver Israel: "I will redeem you with an outstretched arm and with mighty acts of judgment" (6:6). This is the first time in Scripture we meet the word *redeem.* In Israelite culture, a redeemer was someone who was supposed to stand up for the rights of a family member. He would, for example, recover property that had been taken away unjustly, or he would get a relative out of slavery. When God promised to redeem Israel, he

was committing himself to correcting the injustices they suffered. He would act the way they might expect from a close relative. God's promise, then, has a much larger meaning, for his redeeming the Israelites from slavery in Egypt becomes a symbol of his determination to liberate them—and us—from slavery to sin, the Devil, and death.

Pharaoh does not want to release the Israelites, so God unleashes 10 disasters on the Egyptians (chapters 7–12). These plagues dramatize the conflict between the God of Moses and Aaron and the supposed god Pharaoh and his magicians. God says that he is sending the plagues so "The Egyptians shall know that I am the LORD, when I stretch out my hand against Egypt and bring the Israelites out from among them" (7:5). The plagues might have been miracles or they might have been natural phenomena that took place with remarkable timing. In either case, they demonstrate that the God of the Israelites is the real Lord of nature and history.

The plagues seem to be God's response not only to Pharaoh but also to various other gods of Egypt (12:12). For example, the Egyptian sun god, Ra, was supposed to be the source of life and creativity, but he is shown to be powerless against the ninth plague, the deep darkness over the land that threatens the Egyptians with total extinction.

We can see in the demonstration of God's power against Pharaoh a prefiguring of Jesus' ministry. God confronted Pharaoh in a succession of plagues, just as Jesus would confront the evil powers that hold people in bondage to sin and sickness. Jesus overcomes the forces of evil by forgiving sins, healing the sick, freeing people from demonic possession, and even raising the dead. God's show of power in his conflict with Pharaoh points to his more decisive conflict with the powers of sin and death through the suffering and death of his Son.

A Night to Remember

Warm-Up Questions

1 What holidays and observances does your family celebrate?
- ○ Birthdays
- ○ The Fourth of July
- ○ Your parents' wedding anniversary
- ○ Memorial Day, Veterans Day
- ○ Anniversaries of Baptisms and First Communions
- ○ Thanksgiving Day
- ○ The feast day of the saint you're named after
- ○ Other

2 Are there any stories that get told and retold in your family?

What's Happened

Pharaoh and his whole country suffer a series of catastrophes for not allowing the Israelites to offer sacrifice to God in the desert. God prepares a final disaster for the Egyptians but first instructs the Israelites about how to protect themselves and make final preparations to leave Egypt. Jacob's descendants are about to eat their last meal in Egypt and begin their journey to the land God promised to their ancestors.

THE READING

Exodus 12:1–32

The Passover Menu

¹²:¹ The LORD said to Moses and Aaron in the land of Egypt: ² This month shall mark for you the beginning of months; it shall be the first month of the year for you. ³ Tell the whole congregation of Israel that on the tenth of this month they are to take a lamb for each family, a lamb for each household. ⁴ If a household is too small for a whole lamb, it shall join its closest neighbor in obtaining one; the lamb shall be divided in proportion to the number of people who eat of it. ⁵ Your lamb shall be without blemish, a year-old male; you may take it from the sheep or from the goats. ⁶ You shall keep it until the fourteenth day of this month; then the whole assembled congregation of Israel shall slaughter it at twilight. ⁷ They shall take some of the blood and put it on the two doorposts and the lintel of the houses in which they eat it. ⁸ They shall eat the lamb that same night; they shall eat it roasted over the fire with unleavened bread and bitter herbs. . . .

Fast Food

¹¹ This is how you shall eat it: your loins girded, your sandals on your feet, and your staff in your hand; and you shall eat it hurriedly. It is the passover of the LORD. ¹² For I will pass through the land of Egypt that night, and I will strike down every firstborn in the land of Egypt, both human beings and animals; on all the

gods of Egypt I will execute judgments: I am the LORD. [13] The blood shall be a sign for you on the houses where you live: when I see the blood, I will pass over you, and no plague shall destroy you when I strike the land of Egypt.

[14] This day shall be a day of remembrance for you. You shall celebrate it as a festival to the LORD; throughout your generations you shall observe it as a perpetual ordinance.... [17] You shall observe the festival of unleavened bread, for on this very day I brought your companies out of the land of Egypt: you shall observe this day throughout your generations as a perpetual ordinance....

God Passes Over

[21] Then Moses called all the elders of Israel and said to them, "Go, select lambs for your families, and slaughter the passover lamb. [22] Take a bunch of hyssop, dip it in the blood that is in the basin, and touch the lintel and the two doorposts with the blood in the basin. None of you shall go outside the door of your house until morning. [23] For the LORD will pass through to strike down the Egyptians; when he sees the blood on the lintel and on the two doorposts, the LORD will pass over that door and will not allow the destroyer to enter your houses to strike you down. [24] You shall observe this rite as a perpetual ordinance for you and your children. [25] When you come to the land that the LORD will give you, as he has promised, you shall keep this observance. [26] And when your children ask you, 'What do you mean by this observance?' [27] you shall say, 'It is the passover sacrifice to the LORD, for he passed over the houses of the Israelites in Egypt, when he struck down the Egyptians but spared our houses.'" And the people bowed down and worshiped.

[28] The Israelites went and did just as the LORD had commanded Moses and Aaron.

[29] At midnight the LORD struck down all the firstborn in the land of Egypt, from the firstborn of Pharaoh who sat on his throne to the firstborn of the prisoner who was in the dungeon, and all the firstborn of the livestock. [30] Pharaoh arose in the night, he and all his officials and all the Egyptians; and there was a loud cry in Egypt, for there was not a house without someone dead. [31] Then he summoned Moses and Aaron in the night, and said, "Rise up, go away from my people, both you and the Israelites! Go, worship the LORD, as you said. [32] Take your flocks and your herds, as you said, and be gone. And bring a blessing on me too!"

Questions for a Closer Look

1 What was the Israelites' role in the Passover? What was God's role?

2 Which of God's instructions to the Israelites indicate that they are to eat the Passover meal hastily? Why were they to be ready to leave quickly?

3 Reread verses 14, 17, 24–27. Why have these instructions for future celebrations of Passover been woven into the account of the first Passover? Why was it so important for the Israelites to preserve the memory of the Passover (12:24)?

4 What did Moses command the Israelites to do with the lamb's blood? Why?

5 The Passover is a remembrance meal and so is the Eucharist. What similarities do you see between the two celebrations? Look at Matthew 26:17–29 or Luke 22:14–23 as you consider this question.

A Guide to the Reading

The Passover was the climax of God's actions to free the Israelites from their oppressors. God had shown his superiority to Pharaoh with a series of plagues of increasing severity. The 10th and final plague was the death of every firstborn male in Egypt. Only the Israelites escaped the plague of death, because their houses were marked with lamb's blood. "When I see the blood, I will pass over you, and no plague shall destroy you when I strike the land of Egypt" (12:13), God promised his people. The feast is called Passover because it commemorates God's "passing over" the houses of the Israelites.

God directed Moses to establish the Passover feast among the Israelites as an annual occasion to thank God for his deliverance (12:14–20,24–27). By celebrating the Passover every year, each new generation would experience a personal connection to the great events of God's salvation.

Today, more than 3,000 years after the first Passover, Jewish parents still tell their children, "It is because of what the LORD did *for me* when I came out of Egypt" (13:8, emphasis added). The Haggadah is the retelling of the story each year at the Passover meal. The Haggadah describes an event that took place a long time ago, but it is also a contemporary statement. In this way, the past remains alive and present to the Jewish people, and the memory of God's deliverance gives them strength and encouragement for the future.

For Christians, the Passover recalls the roots of faith that we share with our Jewish brothers and sisters. It recalls our common experience of God acting for our salvation. It also prefigures Christ's death and resurrection, which frees men and women from slavery to sin and Satan. Contact with the risen Jesus enabled his followers to begin to understand the meaning of his crucifixion. They saw that the blood he shed was like the blood of the Passover lamb: both had a saving effect. The New Testament asserts that the Passover lamb foreshadowed Christ and helps us understand what Christ accomplished through his death. Peter writes, "You know that you were ransomed from the futile ways inherited from your ancestors, not with perishable things like silver or gold, but with the precious blood of Christ, like that of a lamb without defect or blemish" (1 Peter 1:18–19). In the words of John the Baptist, Jesus is "the Lamb of God who takes away the sin of the world!" (John 1:29).

The death and resurrection of Jesus is the fulfillment of the Passover rite and our true deliverance from bondage. Because it occurred during Passover, the annual celebration of redemption through Jesus has always been associated with that feast. Christians have always celebrated Easter, the feast of Christ's resurrection, as their Passover feast.

Jesus instituted the Eucharist in the course of a Passover meal, and in this way he "gave the Jewish Passover its definitive meaning. Jesus' passing over to his Father by his death and Resurrection, the new Passover, is anticipated in the Supper and celebrated in the Eucharist, which fulfills the Jewish Passover and anticipates the final Passover of the Church in the glory of the kingdom" (*Catechism of the Catholic Church,* section 1340).

Each Mass can be seen as a "little Easter" because the celebration of the Eucharist is a commemoration of Jesus' redemptive death and resurrection. Paul makes this connection between Passover, Easter, and the Eucharist clearer when he uses the imagery of dough and bread to show that our lives have been changed through Christ's sacrifice: "Our paschal lamb, Christ, has been sacrificed. Therefore, let us celebrate the festival, not with the old yeast, the yeast of malice and evil, but with the unleavened bread of sincerity and truth" (1 Corinthians 5:7–8).

Passover will attain its final fulfillment in the messianic kingdom (Luke 22:15–16). When Christ comes again, the freedom from death that is ours through his death and resurrection will be fully manifested. He will bring judgment on all human sin (a judgment prefigured in the plagues of Egypt) and bring his chosen ones into their eternal resting place, the true land of promise.

Questions for Application

1 Picture yourself in a difficult situation. How would you approach God? What would you say to him?

2 This reading from Exodus teaches us about God's concern that we remember and talk about his deeds. Why do you think this is important to God? How important should it be to us?

3 How might a family make commemorative celebrations a greater part of its life? What is something a family could do to strengthen or enrich the celebrations by which it marks anniversaries? Is it worthwhile to write down or record stories of how God has cared for members of the family?

4 How might this reading from Exodus help us understand the Eucharist better? How could this make our participation in the Mass more meaningful?

5 The Israelites were told to prepare and eat the Passover meal quickly. When is it good to act quickly, and when should we take our time and go slowly and deliberately?

6 Reflect on Jesus Christ, the Lamb that was slain, winning deliverance for us from sin and eternal death. How can such a reflection change our outlook on life? How might it affect our behavior?

Approach to Prayer

If you feel comfortable, share with the group experiences you have had of God's intervention in your life. Then take a few minutes, either silently or in conversational prayer, to thank God for the ways he has worked in your life. Conclude by together praying Psalm 105:1–2,45:

> Give thanks to the LORD, call on
>   his name,
>   make known his deeds among
>   the peoples.
> Sing to him, sing praises to him;
>   tell of all his wonderful
>   works. . . .
> Praise the LORD!

——— or ———

Pray Psalm 105, which tells the history of Israel's deliverance from Egypt and expresses thanksgiving for it. As you pray, consider the psalm an expression of your personal "salvation history."

A Living Tradition

Seder Meal

Every year the students at the University of Wisconsin-Superior Newman Center gather for a Seder meal in remembrance of the Passover when the Hebrews were freed from Egypt. In the course of the Seder meal, the students eat many symbolic foods in ritual fashion. The radish reminds them of the bitterness and hardship of the slavery in Egypt. Applesauce, which they use as a substitute for chopped apples, nuts, cinnamon and wine, symbolizes the mortar used by the Hebrew laborers in Egypt. Parsley is eaten as a reminder of springtime, the season of Passover, and as a sign of gratitude to God for the goodness of the earth, for bread and food. They dip the parsley into salt water to symbolize the bitterness Israel endured in its experience of slavery. Each participant eats three small pieces of unleavened bread, the bread that the Israelites ate in Egypt because it had no yeast and therefore took little time to prepare. During the meal each participant drinks four cups of grape juice (in place of wine), representing the four stages by which Israel was delivered from slavery. The red juice is symbolic of the blood the Hebrews sprinkled on their doorposts so that firstborn sons would be passed over. Participants sprinkled 10 drops of juice on their plates to recall the 10 plagues on Egypt. To finish their Seder meal, the Newman students eat a full dinner, which includes lamb and eggs, reminders of the lamb and egg that were offered at the Temple of Jerusalem during the Passover festival.

A large cup and an empty chair are left at the table for the arrival of the precursor of the Messiah. They symbolize hope in the coming of the Kingdom of God.

Paul Birch, the coordinator of the Newman Center, has acted as the leader of the meal, calling the fourth cup, "a reminder of freedom, its hopes, struggles and dreams for so many enslaved nations and individuals. As committed children of God, we are called to witness this precious gift and make it known to all peoples of the earth: those who seek justice, those who lack any rights, and those who fight for freedom."

Between
Discussions

We should feel good about the freeing of the Israelite slaves. But what about the Egyptians? Shouldn't we be troubled or even horrified by the death of all the firstborn Egyptians? Is it true that God destroyed innocent children so that Israel's oppressors could be defeated? There is no simple explanation of this disturbing issue. We can begin, however, by understanding the Old Testament as a record of how people gradually learned about God, who revealed himself a little bit at a time. The Exodus account reflects the mentality of a people who expected God to bring judgment against evil done to them. To their way of thinking, this meant that God would have to punish the entire Egyptian people.

When the Israelites left Egypt, God did not lead them toward the Promised Land by a direct route. One reason was that the nearest highway to Canaan would have taken them along the Mediterranean coast. This would have brought them into contact with Egyptian guards and army units patrolling this busy trade route. The escaping Israelite slaves were in no condition to deal with such powerful forces. The authors write that God thought, "If the people face war, they may change their minds and return to Egypt" (13:17). The Lord understood that the Israelites were afraid, unsure about their newfound freedom, and inexperienced in defending it. He did not want them to lose heart at the beginning of their journey. So God led them by the roundabout way of the wilderness, south toward the Red Sea.

Another reason for the indirect route was strategic. By taking a roundabout way, they might make the Egyptians think that they were confused and disoriented. Then the Egyptians might abandon any plans they had to pursue and destroy the Israelites, figuring that they would perish in the Sinai desert. So God told Moses to have the Israelites turn around and camp by the sea. That way Pharaoh would assume of them, "They are wandering aimlessly in the land; the wilderness has closed in on them" (14:3).

The Israelites pitched camp near the sea, but we are not sure what body of water the author is talking about. Most likely, the Israelites camped near one of the marshy lakes in the eastern Nile Delta, bordering on the wilderness of Sinai and well south of the coastal route.

It did not take the Egyptians long to decide that they had made a mistake in losing their free labor. "When the king of Egypt was told that the people had fled, the minds of Pharaoh and his officials were changed toward the people, and they said, 'What have we done, letting Israel leave our service?'" (14:5). The Egyptian army, with chariots and horses, set off in hot pursuit (14:6–9). Soon Pharaoh's forces were closing in on the Israelites, ready to attack from the rear. With the army at their back and the sea before them, the Israelites had nowhere to turn.

It looked to the Israelites as though their hopes for freedom would be dashed. God had intervened on their behalf, prying them loose from Pharaoh's grip, and that would all be for nothing now. They saw Pharaoh's chariots and cavalry coming at them, and they felt sorry they had ever listened to Moses. It would have been better, they thought, to remain in slavery than to be slaughtered for a few hours' freedom (14:10–12).

God had launched a remarkable campaign for freeing the Israelite slaves. Was it possible that the very same God would now abandon them to the fury of their slave masters? What kind of God would he be to do such a thing? It was God who went out of his way to intervene in the Israelites' situation. The plan he helped them carry out was devised not by the Israelites but by God. If this plan now ended in disaster, God himself would be completely discredited. Is such an outcome possible? The panic-stricken Israelites definitely thought so as they watched in horror, the royal army closing in on them.

The Great Escape

Warm-Up Questions

1 What is the last movie you saw with chase scenes and a last-minute rescue? Which is your favorite such movie? Why?

2 What's the tightest spot you have ever been in? How did you get out of it?

3 Have you or someone you know ever taken part in a rescue operation? What happened? How did everyone feel about it afterward?

Opening the Bible

What's Happened

When the Israelites depart from Egypt after a stay of 430 years (12:40), they go in such haste that the bread dough they take with them does not have time to rise (12:34,39). Pharaoh has finally let them go, and they aren't going to risk any delays! God guides them into the wilderness by his presence in a pillar of cloud by day and a pillar of fire by night (13:18,21). However, as the Israelites probably fear, Pharaoh soon changes his mind about letting them go (14:5–7) and mobilizes his army to go after them.

THE READING

Exodus 14:10–31

In a Tight Spot

14:10 As Pharaoh drew near, the Israelites looked back, and there were the Egyptians advancing on them. In great fear the Israelites cried out to the LORD. 11 They said to Moses, "Was it because there were no graves in Egypt that you have taken us away to die in the wilderness? What have you done to us, bringing us out of Egypt? 12 Is this not the very thing we told you in Egypt, 'Let us alone and let us serve the Egyptians'? For it would have been better for us to serve the Egyptians than to die in the wilderness." 13 But Moses said to the people, "Do not be afraid, stand firm, and see the deliverance that the LORD will accomplish for you today; for the Egyptians whom you see today you shall never see again. 14 The LORD will fight for you, and you have only to keep still."

God Makes a Path Through the Waters

15 Then the LORD said to Moses, "Why do you cry out to me? Tell the Israelites to go forward. 16 But you lift up your staff, and stretch out your hand over the sea and divide it, that the Israelites may go into the sea on dry ground. 17 Then I will harden the hearts of the Egyptians so that they will go in after them; and so I will gain glory for myself over Pharaoh and all his army, his chariots, and his chariot drivers. 18 And the Egyptians shall know

that I am the LORD, when I have gained glory for myself over Pharaoh, his chariots, and his chariot drivers."

¹⁹ The angel of God who was going before the Israelite army moved and went behind them; and the pillar of cloud moved from in front of them and took its place behind them. ²⁰ It came between the army of Egypt and the army of Israel. And so the cloud was there with the darkness, and it lit up the night; one did not come near the other all night.

²¹ Then Moses stretched out his hand over the sea. The LORD drove the sea back by a strong east wind all night, and turned the sea into dry land; and the waters were divided. ²² The Israelites went into the sea on dry ground, the waters forming a wall for them on their right and on their left.

The Sea Path Closes Up

²³ The Egyptians pursued, and went into the sea after them, all of Pharaoh's horses, chariots, and chariot drivers. ²⁴ At the morning watch the LORD in the pillar of fire and cloud looked down upon the Egyptian army, and threw the Egyptian army into panic. ²⁵ He clogged their chariot wheels so that they turned with difficulty. The Egyptians said, "Let us flee from the Israelites, for the LORD is fighting for them against Egypt."

²⁶ Then the LORD said to Moses, "Stretch out your hand over the sea, so that the water may come back upon the Egyptians, upon their chariots and chariot drivers." ²⁷ So Moses stretched out his hand over the sea, and at dawn the sea returned to its normal depth. As the Egyptians fled before it, the LORD tossed the Egyptians into the sea. ²⁸ The waters returned and covered the chariots and the chariot drivers, the entire army of Pharaoh that had followed them into the sea; not one of them remained. ²⁹ But the Israelites walked on dry ground through the sea, the waters forming a wall for them on their right and on their left.

³⁰ Thus the LORD saved Israel that day from the Egyptians; and Israel saw the Egyptians dead on the seashore. ³¹ Israel saw the great work that the LORD did against the Egyptians. So the people feared the LORD and believed in the LORD and in his servant Moses.

Questions for a Closer Look

1 How did the Israelites react to the threat of the Egyptians? How did Moses react? Why did they react differently to the situation?

2 In 14:14 Moses tells the people that they are to "keep still." Yet in the very next verse God has him tell them to "move forward." Is this a contradiction? What did Moses mean by "you have only to keep still"?

3 Locate the verses where Moses' "hand" is mentioned. What did his actions accomplish? How?

4 How did God make himself present to the Israelites in this reading?

5 What were God's reasons for rescuing the Israelites? Cite particular verses in the reading.

A Guide to the Reading

The Israelites were caught between the sea in front of them and the Egyptians behind them. There seemed to be no way out. Their only hope was to trust God and go forward at Moses' command. Sometimes we, too, have to move ahead into the unknown, letting go of what is familiar and secure, and following God's lead into greater freedom.

God miraculously intervened on the Israelites' behalf, opened the sea before them, and provided an escape route. The Lord fulfilled his promise to them: "See the deliverance that the LORD will accomplish for you today; for the Egyptians whom you see today you shall never see again. The LORD will fight for you, and you have only to keep still" (14:13–14). The word *deliverance* here has the broader meaning of salvation. The immediate deliverance would be the Israelites' rescue from the Egyptians, but it would be the start of a greater salvation—a new freedom and a new way of life.

The parting of the waters echoes God's actions in the past. The strong *wind* that parts the *waters* (14:21) brings to mind the *wind* moving over the chaotic *waters* at the moment of creation. It also brings to mind the *wind* that caused the *floodwaters* to abate when God restored creation in the time of Noah (Genesis 1:2; 8:1). By reminding us of God's creative and re-creative actions of the past, the authors help us understand what is taking place as the Israelites flee through the waters. God the Creator is bringing something new into existence—a people who will play a role in his plans for all of humanity.

Looking back on the Exodus more than 1,000 years later, early Church writers would find in this scene many foreshadowings of Christ's death and resurrection. Several Christian writers, for example, saw the wooden staff that God had Moses use to part the waters (14:16) as a prefiguration of Jesus' cross.

The Israelites passed through the sea unharmed; the pursuing Egyptians were drowned. All that the Israelites had to do was cooperate with what God was doing for them. We are challenged in our own struggles to believe that God's grace at work in us accomplishes what we could never do by our own efforts.

The account of the Israelites' safe passage through the Red Sea is read each year during the Easter Vigil. It is given this special place in the Roman Catholic liturgy because it is a chapter in the story of our deliverance. It is a key episode in God's plan of salvation, which was completed by Jesus' death and resurrection.

The Israelites' escape from their enemies and their passing through the waters of the sea are for us a foreshadowing of our own Baptism (1 Corinthians 10:2), which frees us from death and cleanses us of our sins. The Church highlights this symbolism of the waters of the sea in the prayer that follows the reading of the Exodus story at the Easter Vigil: "Lord God, in the new covenant you shed light on the miracles you worked in ancient times: the Red Sea is a symbol of our baptism, and the nation you freed from slavery is a sign of your Christian people. May every nation share the faith and privilege of Israel and come to new birth in the Holy Spirit."

Questions for Application

1 The Israelites' deliverance at the Red Sea is a pivotal event in their national existence. How can significant events change a person's relationship with God? their relationship with other people? their understanding of themselves?

2 The Israelites distrusted God and complained about Moses' leadership. How should young people react when they don't feel good about God's role in their lives? about their parents' role? about their teachers' role?

3 As you reflect on this story of God overcoming the power of sin and evil (symbolized by Pharaoh and his army), what message do you get about God's desire to act in our lives? What means might God use to help free us from bad habits or sinful patterns?

4 The Israelites gained their freedom and became a people, but it was not easy. How can we go about learning to be persistent and determined in pursuing a goal? Would it help to use Moses' advice to the Israelites (14:13-14)?

5 The deliverance at the Red Sea seems to be a story of complete triumph. What can you learn from it about living with health problems, difficulties at school, family tensions, and other difficulties that don't change or, at least, don't change easily?

Approach to Prayer

If you wish, share aloud with the group some ways in which you have experienced freedom thanks to God. Then take a few minutes either silently or in conversational prayer to thank God for the ways he has worked in your life. Conclude by praying together from the Israelites' song of victory at the sea (15:2):

> The LORD is my strength and my
>   might,
> and he has become my
>   salvation;
> this is my God, and I will praise
>   him,
>   my father's God, and I will
>   exalt him.

─── or ───

Pray Exodus 15:1–18, the song the Israelites sang after their deliverance through the sea. As you pray, make the song a personal expression of your own praise and gratitude to God for his action in your life. Conclude with a Glory Be to the Father.

Saints in the Making

You Have Only to Keep Still

Mary Anne Beggs shares her experience of how putting God's word into practice has brought her greater freedom and peace.

My uncle once told me that we were members of the CIA: Catholic, Irish, and alcoholic. Alcoholism is an insidious disease affecting every family member. Each becomes expert at lying (to others and themselves), keeping secrets, and role-playing. In my family, I starred as the "hero" child. From age 11, I assumed adult responsibilities, especially the care and protection of my mother, the nonalcoholic spouse. I always did the right thing. I was a good Catholic daughter, living my faith by fulfilling obligations. In fact, I was downright perfect! But I lived in a state of fear and busyness.

At age 35, during a family crisis, everything changed. Suddenly I could see the lies, secrets, and role-playing as symptoms of disease. And I entered my exile. I cried desperately to return to my secure role, but I could not be that perfect daughter anymore.

Through a diocesan ministry-formation program and some healing retreats, I began to study Scripture and discovered the book of Exodus—in particular Exodus 14:14: "The LORD will fight for you, and you have only to keep still."

I didn't know how to keep still. After a lifetime of trying to maintain calm and order in a family full of storms and chaos, could it be that the answer to my struggles was to just stop doing *and to be still? The paradox attracted me. And the idea moved from my head down to my heart, gradually lifting me out of despair to hope.*

Now, best of all, I am able to be a good but imperfect daughter. And I know that I am God's beloved daughter.

Between Discussions

Passing safely through the water and seeing their enemies swallowed up filled the Israelites with joy. Moses expressed their gratitude at being rescued from certain death in a rousing song. He took no credit himself but glorified God for his wonderful act.

> I will sing to the LORD, for he has triumphed gloriously;
> horse and rider he has thrown into the sea.
> The LORD is my strength and my might,
> and he has become my salvation;
> this is my God, and I will praise him,
> my father's God, and I will exalt him. (15:1–2)

Moses' sister Miriam and the other women accompanied this jubilant song with tambourines and dancing. Imagine how relieved and full of awe the people felt at the wonderful thing God had done for them!

We sing this canticle at the Easter Vigil after hearing read the story of the Israelites' safe passage through the sea. In a celebration of Jesus' victory over sin and death, it makes sense to sing this joyous song of a grateful people celebrating a great victory over death. Singing this hymn helps us look ahead to the time when God's great and final victory will be celebrated as described in the book of Revelation (see Revelation 15:3–4).

When the Israelites entered the sea, they were a disorganized group of refugees. Things began to change when they passed through the sea together, emerging safely with God's help. They started to be formed into a people with a common identity, and their formation continued in stages as they moved through the desert and entered into the Promised Land. The Israelites learned to live in freedom, not needing to be provided for by Pharaoh and also not being oppressed by him. Through this journey they were forged into a nation that learned to know God intimately.

The Israelites made it safely to the other side of the sea, but they had a long way to go before reaching Mount Sinai. They were to worship God there, and, unknown to them at this point, God would offer a covenant to them there. They had an even longer way to go before reaching the land that God has promised to give them. The journey would not be so long in miles, yet it would take 40 years, an awfully long time to be on the road. They did, however, have with them a remarkable sign of God's presence. As they departed from Egypt, "the LORD went in front of them in a pillar of cloud by day, to lead them along the way, and in a pillar of fire by night, to give them light, so that they might travel by day and by night. Neither the pillar of cloud by day nor the pillar of fire by night left its place in front of the people" (13:21–22). This "pillar" of God's presence had already been with the Israelites when it shielded them from the Egyptian army (14:19–20). It would remain with the Israelites until they reached Canaan.

Many spiritual writers have seen a parallel between the Israelites' wandering in the desert and the Christian life, which is very much like a journey. They compare Moses leading the Israelites toward the Promised Land to our heading toward our heavenly home with Christ leading us and showing us the way. They see the cloud and the pillar of fire as symbols of God's grace, protecting us from darkness and keeping us on the path to heaven.

Reading the Exodus story can be an occasion for reflecting on how we have experienced God's presence on our journey through life. It is, after all, God's grace that has blessed us with the gift of faith already, and it will be God's grace that will enable us to keep that faith alive throughout the rest of our lives.

Wonderful Bread

Warm-Up Questions

1 What provisions do you like to take with you on picnics and other outings?

2 How soon before lunch do you start feeling hungry? What effect does being hungry have on you?

3 How would you feel about being in a desert?
- ○ I would enjoy the vast expanse and solitude.
- ○ I would love the sunshine and clear skies.
- ○ I couldn't stand the scorching heat and gritty sand.
- ○ Just thinking about the desert makes me thirsty.

Opening the Bible

What's Happened

After rescuing the Israelites from their slave masters, God leads them through the forbidding wilderness of Sinai, which stretches between the Nile Delta and present-day Israel and Palestine. They travel toward Mount Sinai, apparently in the south of the Sinai wilderness. Although they have just experienced God's dramatic help, they soon begin to complain to Moses and question his— and God's—ability to care for them on this journey.

THE READING

Exodus 16:1–31

"If Only We Had Died . . ."

16:1 The whole congregation of the Israelites set out from Elim; and Israel came to the wilderness of Sin . . . on the fifteenth day of the second month after they had departed from the land of Egypt. 2 The whole congregation of the Israelites complained against Moses and Aaron in the wilderness. 3 The Israelites said to them, "If only we had died by the hand of the LORD in the land of Egypt, when we sat by the fleshpots and ate our fill of bread; for you have brought us out into this wilderness to kill this whole assembly with hunger."

4 Then the LORD said to Moses, "I am going to rain bread from heaven for you, and each day the people shall go out and gather enough for that day. In that way I will test them, whether they will follow my instruction or not. 5 On the sixth day, when they prepare what they bring in, it will be twice as much as they gather on other days." 6 So Moses and Aaron said to all the Israelites, "In the evening you shall know that it was the LORD who brought you out of the land of Egypt, 7 and in the morning you shall see the glory of the LORD, because he has heard your complaining against the LORD. For what are we, that you complain against us?" 8 And Moses said, "When the LORD gives you meat to eat in the evening and your fill of bread in the morning, because the LORD has heard the complaining that you utter against him—what are we? Your complaining is not against us but against the LORD." . . .

"What Is It?"

[13] In the evening quails came up and covered the camp; and in the morning there was a layer of dew around the camp. [14] When the layer of dew lifted, there on the surface of the wilderness was a fine flaky substance, as fine as frost on the ground. [15] When the Israelites saw it, they said to one another, "What is it?" For they did not know what it was. Moses said to them, "It is the bread that the LORD has given you to eat. [16] This is what the LORD has commanded: 'Gather as much of it as each of you needs, an omer to a person according to the number of persons, all providing for those in their own tents.'" [17] The Israelites did so, some gathering more, some less. [18] But when they measured it with an omer, those who gathered much had nothing over, and those who gathered little had no shortage; they gathered as much as each of them needed. . . . [21] Morning by morning they gathered it, as much as each needed; but when the sun grew hot, it melted.

[22] On the sixth day they gathered twice as much food, two omers apiece. When all the leaders of the congregation came and told Moses, [23] he said to them, "This is what the LORD has commanded: 'Tomorrow is a day of solemn rest, a holy sabbath to the LORD; bake what you want to bake and boil what you want to boil, and all that is left over put aside to be kept until morning.'" [24] So they put it aside until morning, as Moses commanded them. . . . [25] Moses said, "Eat it today, for today is a sabbath to the LORD; today you will not find it in the field. [26] Six days you shall gather it; but on the seventh day, which is a sabbath, there will be none."

[27] On the seventh day some of the people went out to gather, and they found none. [28] The LORD said to Moses, "How long will you refuse to keep my commandments and instructions? [29] See! The LORD has given you the sabbath, therefore on the sixth day he gives you food for two days; each of you stay where you are; do not leave your place on the seventh day." [30] So the people rested on the seventh day.

[31] The house of Israel called it manna; it was like coriander seed, white, and the taste of it was like wafers made with honey.

Questions for a Closer Look

1 What do the Israelites' complaints tell us about their attitudes and values?

2 What were the Israelites supposed to learn from the way God answered their complaints?

3 The Israelites seem to want both meat and bread (16:3). Yet the reading focuses on the manna and mentions the quail only briefly. Why is more attention given to the manna? (There is not necessarily one right answer.)

4 In what way did God "test" (16:4) the Israelites? What was this test supposed to teach them? What did the test reveal?

5 In a sentence or two, how would you sum up the message of this reading?

A Guide to the Reading

God fed the Israelites with manna throughout their 40-year journey to the Promised Land (16:35). He had not brought his people into the wilderness to have them die there.

The authors of Exodus never say that there is no natural explanation for the manna. It could have come, for example, from the tamarisk bush, which secretes a sweet resin when it is punctured by a certain insect commonly found there. Or it could have come from the excretions of the insects that feed on the tamarisk fruit. The drops of resin and insect excretions solidify in the cold night air and fall to the ground. They must be gathered up early in the morning because they deteriorate in the heat of the day. Even today, desert Arabs collect this substance and suck it or use it as a sweetener in confectionery. They call it *man,* an Arabic word that corresponds to the Hebrew word *manna.* Whether or not there is a natural explanation for the manna, the authors of Exodus see it as an act of God generously caring for his people. After all, it showed up at just the moment they needed it—and in greater quantities than would normally be expected.

The Israelites were to gather what they needed each day and not save any for the next day. This would show their active faith in God and reliance on him (16:4,19–21). However, they were to gather twice as much on the sixth day so that they could observe the Sabbath rest of the seventh day. This day of rest would remind them that their days of slave labor were over. The tradition in Jewish homes of having two loaves of bread baked in connection with the Friday evening Sabbath meal is a weekly reminder of the miracle of the manna.

Moses reminds the Israelites: "Remember the long way that the LORD your God has led you these forty years in the wilderness, in order to humble you, testing you to know what was in your heart, whether or not you would keep his commandments. He humbled you by letting you hunger, then by feeding you with manna, with which neither you nor your ancestors were acquainted, in order to make you understand that one does not live by bread alone, but by every word that comes from the mouth of the LORD" (Deuteronomy 8:2–3). It was important for the Israelites in the desert to learn obedience to God. When Jesus was fasting in the desert at the start of his public life, Satan tried to deter him from his mission. Jesus used Moses' words to rebuke him: "one does not live by bread alone, but by every word that comes from the mouth of God" (Matthew 4:4).

The book of Wisdom, written perhaps a century before Christ, used the miracle of the manna to encourage the Jews to trust God's goodness. The author reminded his readers that God had nourished the Israelites with "food of angels" and "supplied them from heaven with bread ready to eat, providing every pleasure and suited to every taste" (Wisdom 16:20). Speaking to God, the author of Wisdom marvels that "your sustenance manifested your sweetness toward your children; and the bread, ministering to the desire of the one who took it, was changed to suit everyone's liking" (Wisdom 16:21). He was already familiar with the traditional idea that manna would take on any flavor desired. Jewish rabbis would later teach that the manna assumed whatever taste the eater desired so that each of the Israelites received their favorite dish in the middle of the wilderness.

In the manna we also see a foreshadowing of the Eucharist, which nourishes us on our own pilgrimage through life. Jesus reminded his Jewish listeners, "Your ancestors ate the manna in the wilderness, and they died. . . . I am the living bread that came down from heaven. Whoever eats of this bread will live forever; and the bread that I will give for the life of the world is my flesh" (John 6:49,51). Jesus will sustain us with his own body in the desert of the world until we come into his Promised Land, the heavenly kingdom. The liturgy for the Feast of the Body and Blood of Christ (Corpus Christi) uses the book of Wisdom's words about manna in praise of the Eucharist.

Questions for Application

1 What else besides hunger may have motivated the Israelites to complain in the desert? In what situations do teenagers tend to grumble? At whom do they direct their grumbling? parents? teachers? each other? administrators? God? What message might this reading have for them?

2 Saint Paul encouraged the Corinthians to share their abundance with those in need (2 Corinthians 8:13–14). To underline his point, he reminded them of Exodus 16:18: "Those who gathered much had nothing over, and those who gathered little had no shortage." Why is it important for us to be generous with others?

3 By gathering only enough manna for one day and not storing any of it (16:4,19), the Israelites kept a sense of their need for God. Compare this to what Jesus taught in the Sermon on the Mount (Matthew 6:25–34). What does this petition from the Our Father, "Give us this day our daily bread," tell us about our total dependence on God?

4 Manna nourished the Israelites and gave them strength. Do you think this is the way most Catholics experience the Eucharist? What is something we can do to benefit more from the nourishment provided in the Eucharist?

5 God is intimately concerned with the well-being of the people even though they have trouble trusting in his loving care. How does it affect a person's life to have more trust in God?

Approach to Prayer

Elisabeth Elliot, a missionary and author, wrote, "It is always possible to be thankful for what is given rather than to complain about what is not given. One or the other becomes a habit of life."

With the group, mention a way that God has provided for you. After each blessing, pray this refrain "Give thanks to the LORD, for he is good, for his steadfast love endures forever" (Psalm 136:1). Conclude your time of prayer with the Our Father.

A Living Tradition

Better Than Manna

The theme of the 1976 Eucharistic Congress held in Philadelphia was "The Eucharist and the Hungers of the Human Family." The eight days of the Congress were devoted to eight separate "hungers" and the relationship of the Eucharist to them.

We hunger for God, for if we lack God, it does not matter what else we have. The Eucharist is a special means of overcoming our estrangement from God. We hunger for bread, as the Israelites did in the desert. The Eucharist does not satisfy that hunger, but it does strengthen us for taking part in the struggle against starvation and hunger in the world.

We hunger for freedom and justice, and the Eucharist is a primary source of our commitment to the service of our brothers and sisters. We hunger for the Spirit, who enlivens us in the Eucharist for our work as laity, clergy, and religious.

We hunger for the truth, and in the Eucharist we are committed to the Person Jesus, who proclaimed that he is "the Way, the Truth, and the Life" (John 14:6). We hunger for understanding in a time of estrangement among nations, races, classes, churches, and even generations. The Eucharist promotes reconciliation by bringing us together around the Table of the Lord.

We hunger for peace in a time of violence, terrorism, and war. Christ himself is our peace, and in the Eucharist he provides us with our model and our best hope for peace. Finally, we hunger for Jesus, the Bread of Life. As Jesus said, "if you do not eat the flesh of the Son of Man and drink his blood, you have no life in you" (John 6:53).

God gave the Israelites manna in the desert, satisfying their hunger for food. God addressed their other human hungers as well, giving them a law that would direct them toward becoming a society founded on basic principles of justice. And in the middle of the desert, he addressed their need for God by giving them his own personal name.

Τhe Israelites were challenged in the desert to learn to depend only on God. When they complained about the lack of food, God provided them with manna and quail. When they thirsted, God made water pour forth from a rock (17:1–6). When they ran into enemies who threatened their newfound freedom, God gave them victory through Moses' intercession and Joshua's military prowess (17:8–16). These lessons in trust were hard to learn—and the Israelites weren't straight-A students—but they helped prepare the Israelites for the covenant God would make with them at Mount Sinai.

Many of the psalms (especially Psalms 78, 105, and 106) tell about Israel's experiences. Thus for thousands of years, God's unfailing faithfulness to his people has been recalled in prayer. Praying these psalms today reminds us of the Israelites' struggles to learn reliance on God. It also encourages us to trust the Lord, who is as faithful as ever. Saint Paul told the early Christian believers in Corinth that the Israelites' wilderness experiences "were written down to instruct us" (1 Corinthians 10:11). Israel's desert lesson in trust is the same lesson each of us is still trying to learn today.

Moses led the Israelites first to Mount Sinai and then to Canaan, the land that God had in store for them. They moved in stages, setting up and breaking camp often. By the time they had arrived at Mount Sinai, three months after leaving Egypt, they had set up 10 different campsites (Numbers 33:5–15). Wandering in the desert for the next 40 years, the Israelites broke camp at least 30 times more before crossing the Jordan into Canaan (Numbers 33:16–49).

Few of us have had to pull up stakes that often in our lives. Yet Israel's campsites can be compared to the stages we pass through on life's journey. You can no longer act like elementary school students when you are in high school, and you will act differently in college. Spouses can't continue to live as they did when they were single, nor can parents live as they did before having children. Our responsibilities change as our circumstances or states in life change, and we ourselves change and mature.

When the Israelites left Egypt, God accompanied them as a pillar of cloud by day and of fire by night (13:21–22). This sign was also present at the sea (14:19–20), as well as at Mount Sinai, where the cloud descended on the tent of worship that God had told the people to build (Numbers 9:15). This wondrous sign led them the whole time they were in the desert: "Whenever the cloud was taken up from the tabernacle, the Israelites would set out on each stage of their journey; but if the cloud was not taken up, then they did not set out until the day that it was taken up. For the cloud of the LORD was on the tabernacle by day, and fire was in the cloud by night, before the eyes of all the house of Israel at each stage of their journey" (40:36–38; see also Numbers 9:16–23).

Exodus and Numbers make it clear that the Israelites' journey didn't always mark progress. It included delays, detours, rest stops, forced marches, and occasional rebellions against God. But the journey was a time of learning that the Israelites never forgot. Remembering where we have been, the experiences we have passed through with the Lord, and what we have learned along the way can prepare and equip us also to face the future.

At the Holy Mountain

Warm-Up Questions

1 What formal commitments have your parents entered into?
- ○ Marriage
- ○ Mortgage
- ○ Employment agreement
- ○ Building contract
- ○ Other

2 How did they seal these agreements (for example, exchanging wedding vows and rings, signing a document)?

Opening the Bible

Exodus 19:1–20; 20:1–17; 24:3–8

Camp Sinai

¹⁹:¹ On the third new moon after the Israelites had gone out of the land of Egypt, on that very day, they came into the wilderness of Sinai. ² . . . Israel camped there in front of the mountain. ³ Then Moses went up to God; the LORD called to him from the mountain, saying, "Thus you shall say to the house of Jacob, and tell the Israelites: ⁴ You have seen what I did to the Egyptians, and how I bore you on eagles' wings and brought you to myself. ⁵ Now therefore, if you obey my voice and keep my covenant, you shall be my treasured possession out of all the peoples. Indeed, the whole earth is mine, ⁶ but you shall be for me a priestly kingdom and a holy nation. These are the words that you shall speak to the Israelites."

⁷ So Moses came, summoned the elders of the people, and set before them all these words that the LORD had commanded him. ⁸ The people all answered as one: "Everything that the LORD has spoken we will do." Moses reported the words of the people to the LORD. ⁹ Then the LORD said to Moses, "I am going to come to you in a dense cloud, in order that the people may hear when I speak with you and so trust you ever after."

When Moses had told the words of the people to the LORD, ¹⁰ the LORD said to Moses: "Go to the people and consecrate them today and tomorrow. Have them wash their clothes ¹¹ and prepare for the third day, because on the third day the LORD will come down upon Mount Sinai in the sight of all the people. . . .

Stipulations of the Covenant

¹⁶ On the morning of the third day there was thunder and lightning, as well as a thick cloud on the mountain, and a blast of a trumpet so loud that all the people who were in the camp trembled. ¹⁷ Moses brought the people out of the camp to meet God. They took their stand at the foot of the mountain. ¹⁸ Now Mount Sinai was wrapped in smoke, because the LORD had descended upon it in fire; the smoke went up like the smoke of a kiln, while the whole mountain shook violently. ¹⁹ As the blast of

the trumpet grew louder and louder, Moses would speak and God would answer him in thunder. [20] When the LORD descended upon Mount Sinai, to the top of the mountain, the LORD summoned Moses to the top of the mountain, and Moses went up. . . .

[20:1] Then God spoke all these words:

[2] I am the LORD your God, who brought you out of the land of Egypt, out of the house of slavery; [3] you shall have no other gods before me.

[4] You shall not make for yourself an idol, whether in the form of anything that is in heaven above, or that is on the earth beneath, or that is in the water under the earth. [5] You shall not bow down to them or worship them; for I the LORD your God am a jealous God. . . .

[7] You shall not make wrongful use of the name of the LORD your God. . . .

[8] Remember the sabbath day, and keep it holy. . . .

[12] Honor your father and your mother. . . .

[13] You shall not murder.

[14] You shall not commit adultery.

[15] You shall not steal.

[16] You shall not bear false witness against your neighbor.

[17] You shall not covet your neighbor's house; you shall not covet your neighbor's wife, or male or female slave, or ox, or donkey, or anything that belongs to your neighbor. . . .

The People Agree

[24:3] Moses came and told the people all the words of the LORD and all the ordinances; and all the people answered with one voice, and said, "All the words that the LORD has spoken we will do." [4] And Moses wrote down all the words of the LORD. He rose early in the morning, and built an altar at the foot of the mountain, and set up twelve pillars, corresponding to the twelve tribes of Israel. [5] He sent young men of the people of Israel, who offered burnt offerings and sacrificed oxen as offerings of well-being to the LORD. [6] Moses took half of the blood and put it in basins, and half of the blood he dashed against the altar. [7] Then he took the body of the covenant, and read it in the hearing of the people; and they said, "All that the LORD has spoken we will do, and we will be obedient." [8] Moses took the blood and dashed it on the people, and said, "See the blood of the covenant that the LORD has made with you in accordance with all these words."

Questions for a Closer Look

1 Earlier, God told Moses to bring the people to worship at Mount Sinai (3:12—Sinai is called Horeb in chapter 3). *Do the Israelites worship God at Mount Sinai?*

2 What does it mean to obey God's voice and keep his covenant (19:5)? What is the connection between obeying God's voice and keeping his covenant?

3 What does God promise the people if they keep the covenant (19:5)? How does this promise compare with God's earlier promise (3:8)?

4 A familiar covenant in modern life is marriage. How are the marriage covenant and God's covenant with the Israelites similar? How are they different?

5 Most of the Ten Commandments are stated negatively: "You shall not . . ." How would you state the positive values or behaviors they imply?

6 What is the symbolism of the ceremony that ratifies the covenant (24:3–8)?

A Guide to the Reading

Speaking from the burning bush, God told Moses his name and what his plans were for the rescue of the Israelites from Egypt. Those plans reach their fulfillment now that the Israelites are at Mount Sinai. God had delivered the Israelites as he promised, and now he enters into a special relationship with them. The covenant that he makes through Moses is, in a sense, a new phase of the covenant that he had made centuries before with Abraham and his descendants. A blessed family now becomes a holy nation. God promises to be faithful to Israel, making them his "treasured possession," "a priestly kingdom and a holy nation" (19:5–6). In offering to be Israel's protector, he will be their God, and they will be his people (Deuteronomy 11:22–25; 28:1–14).

As a nation living in intimate relationship with God, Israel will need laws to govern its individual and national life. But the laws they get from God are different from the laws that other nations have. Normally, laws are enforced by the power of the state. Citizens do not have to agree with what the laws stand for as long as they do not break those laws. In the covenant made at Sinai, however, the laws are imposed not by a human government but by God. And God expects more from his people than just observance of the laws. The Israelites understand that they have to do more than just put God's laws into practice, for the laws express the mutual covenant relationship. The laws are intended to show God's people how to imitate God's justice and faithfulness. The people are to obey God's commandments not because they are afraid of God but because they are faithful to him. Their obedience to God's law is a recognition of him as its God, the one God.

God respects the Israelites' new freedom, so he has Moses read the law to the Israelites and ask if they are willing to accept his covenant. All together, as "with one voice," they answer, "All the words that the LORD has spoken we will do" (see 19:7–8; 24:3).

The Ten Commandments and the rest of the covenant code (20:1—23:33) express the Israelites' basic obligations toward God. These obligations flow out of God's revelation of himself. God's covenant people are to live in imitation of God. They are to be faithful and merciful just as God was to them in Egypt.

Faithfulness and justice are to be the foundation of Israel's national existence. Everything about their religious, moral, and social life will be based on those principles. But these commandments are not meant to take away or limit Israel's newfound freedom. Rather they are loving instructions intended to help the Israelites live the full lives that are possible now that they are free.

While the Ten Commandments are mostly phrased in a negative "do not" formula, they express positive values. "You shall not murder" upholds the value of human life. "You shall not steal" implies the right to personal ownership and respect for others' property. The commandments were engraved in stone, as was common in the ancient Near East. The Israelites understood that the laws written "with the finger of God" (31:18) on tablets of stone were for all time and would never change.

After the people accept the law (24:3,7), Moses seals the pact by offering a sacrifice and sprinkling the blood of the sacrificed animals on the people (24:8). Blood symbolizes life, and life belongs to God. Thus sprinkling the blood on the people means they belong to God. They will have to do more than just obey certain precepts. They will have to live as a holy nation, a nation that belongs in a special way to God. At the Last Supper, Jesus will use the term "blood of the covenant" as he institutes the Eucharist, indicating that those who follow him are, by his redeeming blood, fully made into God's holy people.

After the covenant ceremony, Moses and the elders of Israel eat and drink in God's presence on the mountain (24:11). This meal at Sinai cemented the covenant with God. As Christians, we may see in this covenant meal a prefiguration of the Mass, in which we are privileged to partake of the body and blood of Christ, through whom we have a new and deeper covenant with God.

Questions for Application

1 God told the Israelites, "You have seen . . . how I bore you on eagles' wings and brought you to myself" (19:4). What image might you use to describe your experience of God's action in your life?

2 God called Israel a "holy" nation (19:6). Do you think a nation today could be "holy"? What would a holy nation be like?

3 In entering into the covenant with God, the Israelites accepted his laws and commandments (24:7). What do you think of the Ten Commandments and other religious laws? Do they restrict us? liberate us? Explain.

4 What should we do when we become aware that we have neglected our relationship with God? When we disobey God, how can we repair this break in our relationship with him?

5 The Israelites were to worship no other gods or idols (20:3–5). For the Israelites, "other gods" meant pagan idols and deities. What might "other gods" mean to us? What "god" competes with God for our loyalty, energies, resources, and trust? What keeps us from putting God first in our lives? What can we do to reject the temptation to let something other than God take first place in our lives?

6 What is the most important message that you will take from these readings and discussions of Exodus?

Approach to Prayer

Silently, offer a brief prayer of thanksgiving for the new covenant God has made with us in Jesus Christ. Then listen as someone reads the following verses (Hebrews 13:20–21) to close the prayer time:

> May the God of peace, who
> brought back from the dead our
> Lord Jesus, the great shepherd of
> sheep, by the blood of the
> eternal covenant, make you
> complete in everything good so
> that you may do his will,
> working among us that which is
> pleasing in his sight, through
> Jesus Christ, to whom be the
> glory forever and ever. Amen.

———— or ————

Pray Psalm 119:97–112,129–144, which tells of the wonders of God's law. As you pray, resolve to cherish and obey God's commandments. Conclude with a Glory Be to the Father.

A Living Tradition

A Time of Passage

The Israelites marched out of slavery, but they did not enter the Promised Land immediately; they first had to wander in the desert. It is much like the life of a human being. We leave behind our childhood, a time in which we are unable to make many decisions for ourselves. The promised land is adulthood, when we can make our own decisions and are more in control of our lives. But to get from childhood to the promised land of adulthood, we must first pass through the desert of adolescence.

Desert, in this context, must not be looked on negatively. After all, the Hebrews considered their desert experience one of the golden ages of their history. To liken adolescence to the desert experience of the Hebrews is simply to say that it is an in-between time, a time of passage from one stage in life to another. And like any time of passage, it is filled with upheaval, turmoil, change, but also with promise and hope.

The French Dominican theologian, Yves Congar, who was named a cardinal just before he died, had a sense of the wonder of adolescence as a transitional stage in life. He wrote:

Why is youth superabundantly alive, tense with expectation? Because it is meant to grow up and be fertile. It has been compared to a flower not merely because it is bright and fresh, but because it is on the way to a fully developed life and promises fertility. Childhood does not contain the brilliant originality that makes adolescence so attractive; on its slender and less robust stalk, buds are only germinal and flowers remote. Real youth presupposes a more immediate hope; not merely towards possibilities, the accent of original energies, but a move towards direct fertility and the most developed and active forms of life. Youth is life ascending with untapped energies to a life that is perfect and fruit-bearing.

After Words

The Exodus story tells of two central events in the history of Israel: the liberation of the Israelites from slavery in Egypt and their transformation at Mount Sinai into a people belonging to God. Israel would continue to see and understand itself—and God—in light of these events for all succeeding generations. The Exodus was not just a chapter in ancient history. People have continued to rely on the saving power of God that Israel experienced in the Exodus events.

Through these Exodus events, God made himself known to Israel as "I Am." He was a God who cared personally and intimately about his people. I Am heard the Israelites' cries and did not forget them in their misery. He was a God powerful enough to rescue them from oppression, even from the might of Pharaoh's army. I Am took care of them as he led them through the wilderness. Finally, I Am declared himself willing to be their protector, making Israel his chosen people, his holy nation.

God had called and saved Israel to be a people of his own. They were bound to him in a covenant of love and obedience. Yet even before the covenant was fully put into effect, the Israelites broke it by idolatry. They grew tired of waiting for Moses to come down from his meeting with God on the mountain, so they started worshiping a golden calf they had made (chapter 32). Standing between God and his people, Moses made no excuses for the Israelites' unfaithfulness. He did, however, appeal on their behalf to the God who had promised to love his chosen people forever (32:11–13,30–32). So God used Israel's sin as an opportunity to show his love and faithfulness. He delivered them from their own sin just as he had delivered them from Egypt. Moses' pleas moved him, so he told Moses to cut new stone tablets. He was willing to restore his covenant relationship with Israel and to renew his promises to them—in other words, he was willing to forgive. Just as Moses interceded with God on behalf of his sinful people, so Christ would be the final and enduring mediator between God and humankind.

God taught Moses about himself on Mount Sinai. God said that he is "the LORD, the LORD, a God merciful and gracious, slow to anger, and abounding in steadfast love and faithfulness" (34:6). Israel was judged not with harshness but with mercy.

The closing chapters of the book of Deuteronomy describe what happened when Moses was about to die. With the few Israelites who had survived the 40 years in the desert and with the large new generation born during those years, Moses renewed the Sinai covenant. He reminded them as they were about to enter the Promised Land that their parents had promised at Sinai to be faithful to God. Then he climbed Mount Pisgah, just east of the Jordan River (in present-day Jordan), and the Lord showed him all the land that he had sworn to give to Abraham and his descendants. At the age of 120, Moses died there in sight of the Promised Land, and the people of Israel mourned him (Deuteronomy 34:7–8).

We can compare our life as Christians to the story of the Israelites. They were freed from slavery in Egypt through the blood of the Passover lamb and they escaped through the sea; we have been freed from enslavement to sin and Satan by Christ's death and resurrection. God reached out to the Israelites in their moments of need and lack of faith; God reaches out to us in the same way. God renewed his covenant with the Israelites after they sinned against him; God is constantly renewing his covenant with us in Christ, offering forgiveness, because God is true to his nature: gracious, merciful, and steadfast in love.

Homeward Bound

The book of Exodus tells the story of an extraordinary journey—a journey out from Egypt through a desert wilderness, first to Mount Sinai and then to the Promised Land of Canaan, a land flowing with milk and honey. But the Exodus story is not the only travel story in the Bible. In fact, the Bible is full of stories about men and women who set out on unusual journeys. God told Abraham to leave his country and family and go to a new land (Genesis 12:1). Jacob and his family went to Egypt for relief from famine (Genesis 46). When Jerusalem fell in 587 B.C., many of the survivors made the long trek into exile in Babylon (2 Kings 25:8–12). Mary hastened from Nazareth to the hill country of Judah to visit Elizabeth (Luke 1:39–40). Joseph, Mary, and Jesus fled to Egypt to escape Herod's wrath (Matthew 2:13–15). Luke devotes about 10 chapters to describing Jesus' journey to Jerusalem, where he would die.

Each of these stories teaches us something about the stages we pass through in our lives as Christians. Abraham left his home to go to a new, unknown land. We, too, are often challenged by God to make our way into new territory. The Israelites escaped from their slavery in Egypt by passing through the waters of the sea into a new life of freedom. In the same way, we are freed from sin and receive new life in Christ through the waters of Baptism. And just as Jesus went the way of the cross, so must we follow him on that path.

The New Testament letter to the Hebrews describes Abraham and Moses and the generations that went before them in faith as "strangers and foreigners on the earth . . . seeking a homeland" (Hebrews 11:13–14). The letter says that Abraham "looked forward to the city . . . whose architect and builder is God" (Hebrews 11:10). Departing from Egypt, Moses "persevered as though he saw him who is invisible" (Hebrews 11:27). Later spiritual writers often compared our earthly life to a journey. They urged us to keep our eyes fixed on heaven as our final goal:

"Here we have no lasting city, but we are looking for the city that is to come" (Hebrews 13:14).

Saint Cyprian of Carthage, a third-century bishop in North Africa and a father of the Church, echoed the author of Hebrews:

> We are living here now as aliens and only for a time. When the day of our homecoming puts an end to our exile, frees us from the bonds of the world, and restores us to paradise and to a kingdom, we should welcome it. What man, stationed in a foreign land, would not want to return to his own country as soon as possible? Well, we look upon paradise as our country, and a great crowd of our loved ones awaits us there.

Similarly, Saint Augustine of Hippo (354–430) wrote, "We are but travelers on a journey without as yet a fixed residence; we are on our way, not yet in our native land. We are in a state of longing, not yet of enjoyment. But let us continue on our way, and continue without laziness or delay, so that we may ultimately arrive at our destination." Centuries later the French pastor Saint John Vianney (1786–1859) expressed the same point more simply: "Our home is—heaven. On earth we are like travelers staying in a hotel. When one is away, one is always thinking of going home."

You may hold a passport issued by the government that declares you a citizen of the United States, but the reality is that, as a Christian, your eternal citizenship is in heaven (see Philippians 3:20). This earth, full of joys and sufferings, blessings and temptations, is not your permanent home. As Christians, the author of Hebrews declares, we "desire a better country, that is, a heavenly one" (Hebrews 11:16). Just like the Israelites journeying to Canaan, we are on a journey; we are "pilgrims" simply "passing through" en route to our true homeland.

The word *pilgrim* comes from Latin roots meaning "stranger" passing "through a field." A traveler is one who goes through a territory and crosses a frontier. The traveler thus becomes a stranger, a pilgrim, leaving the familiar behind, heading toward a new land.

A pilgrim may be a stranger, but he or she has a purpose or destination in traveling. A pilgrim does not simply meander. To meander is to wander aimlessly, to go around in circles. The pilgrim leaves from a specific place, follows a specific route, and arrives at a specific point. Pilgrims know exactly where they are headed. Pilgrims and travelers are often asked, "Where are you going?" The only answer we can give as Christians is "Home to heaven."

Ever since Adam and Eve's exile from the Garden of Eden, humans have yearned to return to the innocent union with God for which we were created. Because of this, we have called heaven our homeland, our heart's deepest longing. As much as we love this earth as God's gift to us, we are homesick for heaven.

The *Catechism of the Catholic Church* states that "heaven is the ultimate end and fulfillment of the deepest human longings, the state of supreme, definitive happiness" (section 1024). It affirms that "those who die in God's grace and friendship and are perfectly purified live for ever with Christ" (section 1023).

Our Exodus reading has helped us understand how life is a journey toward the Promised Land, a journey home to heaven. We need to take time on this journey to ask ourselves what it means for us to live as strangers and foreigners in this present world. Do the "things that are on earth" satisfy us and make us happy, or are our minds set on "things that are above" (Colossians 3:2)? Are we meandering? Do we need to get back on track? Do we really want to come to the end of our pilgrimage and reach our final destination?

Our life journey gets hard at times, and it can be so long and demanding that it tires us out. We can pick up our spirits by fostering the hope of heaven within us and reflecting on the joys that await us there. Keeping our hearts fixed on our destination can help us make it through rough times.

Imagine how happy the Israelites must have been when they finally ended their long journey and crossed the Jordan River into the Promised Land. Our own joy will be far greater when we reach our heavenly homeland. While we are still on the way, let's remember that "we are Christ's pilgrim people, journeying until we reach our homeland, singing on the way as we eagerly expect the fulfillment of our hope, for if one hopes, even though his tongue is still, he is singing always in his heart" (Advent Responsory, *The Liturgy of the Hours*).

The New Moses

The events of Exodus pointed the way to our redemption in Christ. In the blood of the lamb that the Israelites smeared over their doors, the early Christians saw a prefigurement of the saving power of Christ's blood shed on the cross. We see the manna in the desert as a prefiguring of the Eucharist. There is another important foreshadowing that we should examine. As Israel's great liberator and mediator with God, Moses foreshadows Jesus, who is our liberator from sin and our reconciler with the Father. In fact, Moses himself seemed to realize that he was the forerunner of one yet to come, for he told the people of Israel, "The LORD your God will raise up for you a prophet like me from among your own people; you shall heed such a prophet" (Deuteronomy 18:15). The earliest Christians understood that Moses' prediction was fulfilled in Jesus. Both Peter and Stephen quote Deuteronomy 18:15, relating it directly to Jesus (Acts 3:22; 7:37).

This understanding of Jesus as the "new Moses" is particularly obvious in the Gospel of John. When Philip tells Nathanael about his meeting with Jesus, Philip says, "We have found him about whom Moses in the law and also the prophets wrote, Jesus son of Joseph from Nazareth" (John 1:45). And when the people saw Jesus multiply bread and fish, "they began to say, 'This is indeed the prophet who is to come into the world'" (John 6:14). Moreover, Jesus applied Moses' prophetic words recorded in Deuteronomy 18:15 to himself. He told Jews who failed to believe in him, "Do not think that I will accuse you before the Father; your accuser is Moses, on whom you have set your hope. If you believed Moses, you would believe me, *for he wrote about me*" (John 5:45–46; italics mine).

We can detect in the Gospels many similarities between Moses and Jesus. They were both born into a people suffering under repressive rule. They were both saved as infants from being murdered by tyrannical kings. They both spent time in the desert preparing for their missions: Moses as a shepherd in Midian for 40 years, Jesus in his 40-day fast in the desert preparing for his public ministry. Moses brought the Ten Commandments down from Mount Sinai to the Israelites; in the Sermon on the Mount Jesus interpreted the law for his followers, pointing out its fundamental principle of love and its goal in the Kingdom of God. Both Moses and Jesus were frequently misunderstood by those nearest to them as they carried out God's plan of deliverance.

The letter to the Hebrews shows how Moses' life anticipated Jesus. Comparing Jesus as mediator of a new covenant with Moses as mediator of the old covenant, it shows how much greater Jesus was. "Now Moses was faithful in all God's house as a servant, to testify to the things that would be spoken later. Christ, however, was faithful over God's house as a son" (Hebrews 3:5–6).

The Fathers of the Church saw in the Old Testament a record of the first stages of God's plan for our salvation. They looked for similarities between the Old and New Testaments because they considered both books to be part of the same plan. Their alertness to Old Testament signs of things to come enabled them to spot many shadows and reflections that appeared as clues of the plan that eventually unfolded in the coming of Christ, who perfectly fulfills God's plan.

These ancient Christian writers wanted to show that Jesus was the one who brought God's dealings with Israel to fulfillment. They also wanted to help Christian readers see the Exodus accounts as pointing toward God's presence among them through Christ and the Spirit. The book of Exodus provided Christians with images that helped them understand their own experience as Christians.

A homily of Saint John Chrysostom (c. 347–407) offers an example of this pastoral concern:

> The Israelites witnessed marvels; you also will witness marvels, greater and more splendid than those which accompanied them on their departure from Egypt. You did not see Pharaoh drowned with his armies, but you have seen the devil with his weapons overcome by the waters of

baptism. The Israelites passed through the sea; you have passed from death to life. They were delivered from the Egyptians; you have been delivered from the powers of darkness. The Israelites were freed from slavery to a pagan people; you have been freed from the much greater slavery to sin.

Do you need another argument to show that the gifts you have received are greater than theirs? The Israelites could not look on the face of Moses in glory, though he was their fellow servant and kinsman. But you have seen the face of Christ in his glory. Paul cried out: We see the glory of the Lord with faces unveiled.

In those days Christ was present to the Israelites as he followed them, but he is present to us in a much deeper sense. . . . After Egypt they dwelt in desert places; after your departure you will dwell in heaven. Their great leader and commander was Moses; we have a new Moses, God himself as our leader and commander.

What distinguished the first Moses? Moses, *Scripture tells us,* was more gentle than all who dwelt upon the earth. *We can rightly say the same of the new Moses, for there was with him the very Spirit of gentleness, united to him in his inmost being. In those days Moses raised his hands to heaven and brought down manna, the bread of angels; the new Moses raises his hands to heaven and gives us the food of eternal life. Moses struck the rock and brought forth streams of water; Christ touches his table [the altar in the church], strikes the spiritual rock of the new covenant, and draws forth the living water of the Spirit. This rock is like a fountain in the midst of Christ's table, so that on all sides the flocks may draw near to this living spring and refresh themselves in the waters of salvation.*

We can learn from the example of the ancient Christians, applying the lessons of the Exodus story to our own circumstances. The issues raised in the gigantic struggle between the Egyptians and the Israelites are issues that are important for us now and will remain important for us throughout our lives. How are we to deal with abuse of power? How much should we rely on ourselves, and how much should we rely on God? How much does God really care about us? How important is it for us to stick together as God's people? Where are we headed in our lives? What does it really mean to be free? How important are commitments? What are the consequences of faithfulness and unfaithfulness to our commitments?

Exodus does not give the final answer to any of these questions, but it can get us started on our lifelong search for answers.

Listening When God Speaks

As you have worked your way through this book, you have been listening to God's word. But this is not the first time that God has spoken to you, and indeed God has been speaking to you throughout your young life. Let's look at some of the ways in which God speaks to you, and let's look at some of the ways in which you can improve your listening skills

The most obvious way in which you receive messages from God is through the Scripture, which is the Word of God. The people of Israel and the early Christians recorded their experiences of God's saving acts in history, and our religious tradition accepts their writings as God's Word to us. We believe that when we read Scripture, or hear it read, God is communicating his Word to us. It would be a good thing for you to develop the habit of reading the Bible on a regular basis, and you should make every effort to benefit from the weekly reading of Scripture at Mass.

An excellent way in which to listen to God speaking to us in Scripture is to pray the Scripture. Begin by adopting a proper prayer *posture* through the selection of an appropriate time and place for prayer. Once in the proper posture, become aware of God's *presence* in your life and in the time and place you have chosen for your prayer. Then *pray* for guidance from the Holy Spirit, asking help to understand the passage you will be reading and reflecting on. You are now ready to read your selected *passage,* but you must read slowly and deliberately, with the intention of hearing God's voice in the passage. After you have read and reread the passage, *pause* for reflection on the passage. Allow time for God to speak to you through the words of the text.

The Bible is the Word of God, but it is not the only Word of God. Jesus Christ is also the Word of God, the Word made flesh. The Gospel of John begins with that message: "In the beginning was the Word, and the Word was with God, and the Word was

God. . . . And the Word became flesh and made his dwelling among us." We want, then, to listen to God speaking to us in Jesus Christ and one good way to do that is by participating fully in Mass. Gathering together with the other worshipers, we enter into communion with them and with the presiding priest. The words and actions of the celebration put our spirits at rest, so that by the time we enter into communion with Christ in the Eucharist, we are in a position to hear God's message of love, peace, and salvation. We should not make the mistake of thinking that Jesus speaks to us only at the moment of receiving the Eucharist. His voice can be heard—if only we listen—through the community, through the priest, through the entire Eucharistic celebration, and finally, bringing it all together, in the eating and drinking of the Body and Blood of Christ.

Because the Church is the Body of Christ, we can also speak of the Church as the Word of God. God speaks to us through the community of believers, and in a special way through the leadership of that community. One way to listen to the voice of God in the Church is by paying attention to the voices of the believers nearest us: our parents and teachers, our parish priest, and the people we worship with on Sunday. Another way is to stay in touch with what the leadership of our Church is teaching. The bishops of our Church, especially the bishop of Rome, the Holy Father, and our own local bishop, the leader of the Church where we are active, speak to us in words that have the authority of the Word of God, and as Catholics we hear in them the voice of God.

Finally, God speaks to us in our own life experiences. The Second Vatican Council recovered the biblical image of "reading the signs of the times," that is, hearing the voice of God in the events of history. On the personal level, we can hear God speaking to us in such things as our encounters with others, our decisions, our successes and failures, and the challenges arising from the difficulties of life. To hear God's voice in our life experiences, we need to pay attention to those experiences, reflect on them, and learn from them.

There is a wonderful story in the Old Testament about a young boy named Samuel. (You can read it in 1 Samuel 3.) Samuel was assisting an old priest named Eli, who was waiting in the temple for God to speak to him. One night while he was sleeping, Samuel heard someone call him. He assumed it was Eli, so he went and woke Eli up to find out what he wanted. Eli responded that he had not called, and he sent the boy back to bed. After a while Samuel heard his name called again, but once more Eli told the boy that it was not him. When it happened a third time, Eli knew that it was God calling to Samuel and he said to the boy, "Go to sleep, and if you are called, reply, 'Speak, LORD, for your servant is listening.'"

The first thing to notice about this story is that everybody expected God to speak to the old priest, but God spoke to the young boy instead. It is important that you be receptive in your youth to the voice of God and not think that God will only speak to you "later." God is speaking to you now—in the Scriptures, in Jesus Christ, in the Church, and in your life experiences.

The other point of the story is that, in order to hear God speaking to us, we must be listening. Samuel would never have received God's message if he had not listened, and the same thing applies to us. Ours is a busy life, with plenty of noise. We need to learn how to cut through all the noise and listen to God speaking to us.

Resources

Bibles

The following editions of the Bible contain the full set of biblical books recognized by the Catholic Church, along with a great deal of useful explanatory material:

➤ The Catholic Youth Bible (Saint Mary's Press), which can be ordered with either the New American Bible or the New Revised Standard Version

➤ Student Bible for Catholics (Thomas Nelson Publishers), which uses the text of the New American Bible

➤ The Catholic Study Bible (Oxford University Press), which uses the text of the New American Bible

➤ The Catholic Bible: Personal Study Edition (Oxford University Press), which also uses the text of the New American Bible

Additional Sources

➤ Craghan, John F. *Exodus*. Collegeville, MN: Liturgical Press, 1985.

➤ Daley, Michael J. "Make Your Own Exodus This Lent," *Youth Update*, Cincinnati, OH: St. Anthony Messenger Press, February 2000.